D1389316

# EIGHT BELLS

—— & ——

# TOP MASTS

# EIGHT BELLS
## &
# TOP MASTS

DIARIES FROM A TRAMP STEAMER

CHRISTOPHER LEE

HEADLINE

First published in 2001
by HEADLINE BOOK PUBLISHING

Christopher Lee would be happy to hear from readers with their
comments on the book at the following e-mail address:
lee@sceptredisle.demon.co.uk

10 9 8 7 6 5 4 3 2 1

British Library Cataloguing in Publication Data

Lee, Christopher
Eight bells and top masts
1. Lee, Christopher 2. Great Britain
I. Title
941'.082'092

ISBN 0 7472 7492 4

Typeset by Avon Dataset Ltd, Bidford-on-Avon, Warks
Designed by Jane Coney

Printed and bound in Great Britain by
Clays Ltd, St Ives plc, Bungay, Suffolk

HEADLINE BOOK PUBLISHING
A division of Hodder Headline
338 Euston Road
London NW1 3BH

www.headline.co.uk
www.hodderheadline.com

For
James Eamon MacCobb
Master Mariner

# CONTENTS

From a distance, The Tramp looked a pretty ship –
from a distance

# AUTHOR'S NOTE

This is the story of an old tramp, a hobo, but not a bum. It is the tale of a steamship that tramped from port to port, never quite knowing where the next cargo might be or what it would be, or where it would be taken. A universal carrier grubbing for trade.

It is, too, the story of a young lad who simply wanted to go to sea. He wanted to tie knots, to splice and bend ropes. He wanted the smell of a ship and the rattle of an anchor running out in a foreign sound. He wanted the solitude of horizons. He was a loner who instinctively sought the company of a ship rather than fellows. He and The Tramp became firm friends.

She was the last of a breed. She was built in 1942 at the Caledon Yard in Dundee. Her engines were from North Eastern Marine on the Tyne, where his mother's family of Scottish engineers had worked. In Dundee they'd riveted her hull together in double-quick time. In those frightening war years, with ships being sunk each day by German

U-boats and mines, every available vessel was needed to put to sea as quickly as possible. The Americans were saying they could weld together a prefabricated Liberty ship in forty-eight hours. Perhaps they could. But even though there was a war on, the old northern and Caledonian yards preserved what they thought was a standard of proper British shipbuilding. No welding for them. Big, fat, strong rivets. And, by the by, never admit the Americans knew more about welding than the British. In 1942, the year before the lad was born, she went to sea as the *Empire Heywood*. She got the name because she was an empire class – a sort of Morris Oxford of the maritime world. Five hatches, three masts, triple engines, one propeller and one funnel. Solid, reliable and reasonably comfortable. She was built to last just as long as the war did. There were 277 of them. The Germans managed to sink seventy. They missed this one.

And so she fetched supplies from anywhere they might be found, from Galveston to Liverpool, Cape Town to the Tyne, Charleston to Grangemouth, Baltimore to Swansea. As she sailed the southern oceans and the Atlantic, the packs of German U-boats waited. She was lucky. Just. More than the price of oil in a beleaguered Britain was indeed raised by more than a penny a gallon.*

And when that terrible war was done, the ship that was built for the duration was tied up and abandoned until, that is, she was bought for nothing at all. Her owners went down to the docks, found a Liverpool master who'd thought himself finished, a Glaswegian engineer and a handful of odds and sods, some on the way up, others who were not. They sent this motley crew to sea, to fetch a cargo of

---

*Philip Zec, the political cartoonist in the *Daily Mirror*, in March 1942 depicted a dying merchant seaman clinging to the wreckage from his torpedoed tanker. His caption was the government announcement of that previous day: 'The price of petrol has been increased by 1d – official'.

beans from somewhere. Phosphate from there, sugar from another place. Maybe five hatches of scrap. After that war, there was plenty of scrap.

Soon she was bought by a trader with honourable parchments, an old shipping company with mahogany and high-stooled offices in the City of London, and one or two partners in spats.

She had begun life as a coal-burner. Now, her bunkers were removed and replaced by oil tanks, her boilers converted, although not on the Tyne, or on the Clyde. She was sailed to Deutsche Werft in Hamburg. She was given a good home, a good name and a good crew of Hong Kong Chinese and British mates and engineers.

For more than a decade she earned her owners a living. As the 1950s came to a close, so did an era in British shipping. Tramping was running its time. When, one January morning in 1958, a young lad from the Kent marshes signed her articles, he could never have known he had joined a dying ship, a dying way of life.

Faithfully, for nigh on two years the lad recorded what he saw, what he felt and what he did. It was all written, sometimes carefully, sometimes not, in school notebooks. He sketched when he could not describe in words the moments of magic and the moments of fear. A couple of those books survived.

At the end of each four-hour watch, the bridge bell is struck eight times. Eight bells, all change. The Tramp is the story of an era of mighty change. At sea, the closing of a proud history. On land, the end of a sometimes not-so-proud colonial age. As she and the lad left successive harbours, many an old ensign was being struck, not on her poop deck but from sturdier jackstaffs ashore. The wind of change. The end of colonial rule. This, then, is the lad's own awakening in a way of life that he'd thought was for ever, more or less as he sketched in his log of the last circumnavigation of The Tramp.

None of the names of the people in this book is real. The laws of libel are not that easy and, anyway, why upset people? But their characters are real enough. They are a mixture of the masters, mates, engineers and crew who sailed with that lad during what became two long voyages and one short one. So what follows is part-fact and part-fiction – just like real life.

# 1

## THE TRAMP

A slate-cloud Thames morning, late August, that time when sleeping optimists never believe that autumn is getting ready. Barely-awake workers, damp hand-rolled cigarettes pasted and dangling from silent lips, lean against the rail of the Woolwich ferry, its great paddles churning ochre wakes from the ancient river. Dockers. Wharfies. Tallymen. Big boots. Caps. Sullen morning faces. Across the black waters of the Royal Docks are row upon row of cargo ships, arm-thick hawsers and hemps looped to iron bollards beneath the stark lattices of silent cranes.

Black-hulled British India steamers. Red-banded funnels of the Clan boats. An away-from-home Blue Funnel. The high-sided Lykes Lines with company name in spindly twenty-foot letters along her hull; the *Stars and Stripes* still in the first light. The clear, clean blue Maersk with general cargo from Rotterdam. Ben Bros. Ellermans. Federal. The *Maru* from Osaka. The *Gothic*, on a brief visit and making ready for New Zealand. The Bank boat with its sand-coloured superstructure not quite dry, but set for Singapore.

At the end, near the lock gates, The Tramp, riveted together in a few days, just for the duration of the war, but ten years later still here. Moored alongside her, a sturdy broad-beamed barge. But this is no rusty and menacing lighter to be tugged upstream to a Mortlake jetty. This is a strong wooden-hulled Thames sailing barge. Thick spruce mast and spars up and along which will soon rattle the hoops and blocks that hoist the tan gaff-rigged canvases. In an hour the wharfies will be aboard The Tramp. The steam winches will hiss and clank. Strops of jute bales of Havana sugar will be hoisted from her great hold and swung over the sheer black and rust side and down to the open hatch of the barge until she's taken her fill. Then she'll be off. No Santiago, Calcutta, Cape Town or Kobe for her. Out through the lock and into the ebb until Long Reach, then tacking from Charlton, Erith and Dartford, Gravesend and Tilbury, and by morning off the Whitstable sticks and alongside again, and maybe peas and pie in Rosie's Cafe. Rosie's Cafe, not Café. Frank Bevan the skipper, Billie the mate on loan, on a promise, from the reform school, and a scuff-shoed lad from the marshes along the Lower Reach.

As the barge slips into the stream and the paddle ferry waits for her to settle past, the lad will look back at the cream masts and booms, the white bridge deck and that red, white and black funnel. In a couple of years he'll have had his spell in the barge. He'll be wanting other horizons, and he'll be stowing his gear as apprentice boy aboard that same ship, though yet he doesn't know it. Can't know it. A couple of years? An age away. Not yet a first kiss. But for now there's the tarpaulin to stretch, the hatch irons to drop into their slots, the hammer to be taken to the wedges. There's not much time.

It is the late 1950s. What the lad doesn't know is that time is closing in on the skipper, the barge, the tug that brought them through the lock, even on the Royal Docks themselves, the Royal Victoria and the King George V, even on the mighty-sided ships alongside with busy derricks, mates and masters, bosuns and greasers, wharfies and tallymen. For now is the lingering death of The Tramp. When she is gone, her end will ring the end of the ancient trade when an old converted coal-burner with Hong Kong Chinese crew and a few British officers would tramp from port to port, picking up cargo where she could. Never knowing where she, and they, would be heading next. The scruff end of the merchant fleet. A master with a flat cap. A Second Mate with one lung. A Third Mate without a ticket.* An ageing ex-policeman as Fourth Engineer. A far cry from the liveried elegance of the P&O liner moored at the smarter end of the pier. In those late 1950s, all was changing, but it was the traditional tramping trade that was about to disappear.

## 13 AUGUST 1956

We're in the KG 5, alongside some old tramp. Tide was a right bugger getting cross the Charlton. Frank didn't want a tug, but he knew he had to. A Sun tug, she was. He says they're the best. We tied abeam and she took us through the lock just after three and we were moored up by half-past. The Tramp's a nice old girl.

*Merchant Navy slang for what was then the Board of Trade Certificates of Competence. There were two levels – foreign and home trade – and deck officers were examined at three levels: Second Mate, Mate (aboard ships sometimes called Chief Officer) and Master Mariner (sometimes called Captain). There was an Extra Master certificate, but it was not necessary for command. Having a Master's 'ticket' was by no means a guarantee of command, and many holders sailed as Second Mate and Mate simply because they needed more experience and, if staying with one company, were subject to the normal promotion process of numbers of commands available.

Had a look at her as we came in. Bit rusty, but not as bad as some of them. Frank said she was a coal-burner one time, and after the war a couple of London Greeks bought her. Don't see her much in London. Mostly she's away couple of years at least. The Second Mate's Scotch and he came down for a brew. The Jacob's really wobbly and he nearly came a cropper jumping aboard. When I looked up, there's all these Chinkies looking down laughing their funny heads off. They all got gold teeth. Frank reckons they have their teeth taken out and gold ones put in for when they need the money. The Second Mate says they're OK enough. No trouble, not like the Liverpool crowd he sailed with on his last ship. One of the apprentices come down when we stopped loading. Said his dad had sailed in an Everard barge out of Maldon before the war. Frank said he knew him. Reckoned he was a good sailorman. Wouldn't mind being an apprentice. It'd be nice to go deep sea. Maybe one day.

'Maybe one day' soon arrived. He'd been told he was bound not for Rio but the factory. Get a trade, they'd told him, get a trade. Clock on for a job for life. Horizons? Every year he'd have them. Two weeks at Broadstairs. So much sifted sand that there was not even a flat stone to skim across the breaking waves to whatever lay beyond. He was not a rebel. Strong will was enough. The parents knew him better than he did. They'd fret, but they'd let him go or they'd lose him for ever, not just between eight and five Mondays to Fridays.

He'll be gone from home for close on two years. No Whitstable, Faversham, Mersea, Pinmill and Maldon. He'll be bound for Bombay, Madras, the Yangste, Tientsin, Ngoya, Eureka, Nauru, Sydney, North Bend, Panama, Galveston, Havana. The true tramp steamer rarely touched the northern line of ports from Brest to Kiel. They were considered home waters, and a crew could sign off the ship's articles and demand to be sent home.

Therefore he will have to get used to this 7,000 tons of ship being his home in every sense.

He will learn to stow salt from the Sudan, scrap from Texas, bags of sugar from Havana, hills of phosphate from Nauru. He will learn the names and customs of the bars from Shaukiwan, and Mojiko to Pensacola, São Paulo and Bahía Blanca, Boogie Street to Ma Gleeson's. He will be nervous in the company of tall, languid Sudanese. He will be fascinated by the Egyptian gully-gully man with his day-old chicks disappearing into cuffs and sleeves as deftly do the lad's shillings. He will smell his first Madrasi slums, ride in his first rickshaw and hang from the Wanchai tram. He will yearn for a letter from home and forget to write. In the daytime he will chip and paint the decks. Climb, for the first time, the tall swaying foremast. Throw the long black handles of the aged steam winches as the derricks haul iron beams from the 'tween deck hatches. The lad will learn to scrub for cockroaches. That done, he'll listen to trampers' tales as, long past midnight, he stands lookout across the summer Pacific. He will learn to live in the company of older men, men who sometimes frighten, others who laugh, others who sadden. Men who will go down in the memory with their ship. For just as The Tramp is dying, so too are the Mates, the engineers, the deckhands, greasers, donkeymen and boilermen, the bosuns and casabs who sail her.

MacAuley, the hugely bewhiskered Mate who once designed shoes. Brown, the dour engineer who cries himself to sleep most nights in the arms of his Chinese boy. Butrell, the Yorkshire skipper who puts on his bowler hat when entering and leaving port. Langtry, the minor aristocrat with his suede shoes and his pocket of peppermint creams. Wilson, who washes his hair but once a quarter-day and keeps a snake in his locker. Butler, who plans to sail the world in a small boat and writes mysterious letters to a South Sea Islands chief. Chong Ah Ping, the carpenter who sends all his money home to his two wives in Kowloon. Fan Kan, who disappears like a ghostly spy wherever the ship comes alongside. Bevan, who once was a priest and is now a rutting Second Mate. Ainslie, the other apprentice. A mixture of all the lad never knew.

These are his new tutors, his models. He has no peers. Betters, yes. Peers, no. His friends are his exercise books. Books for his navigation, his seamanship, his ship construction lessons. But he takes few notes of formal instruction. He is a poor pupil but a careful learner.

For nearly two years, in those exercise books, he tells what he sees and hears about her decks, compartments, ladders, monkey island, bridge, wireless shack and chartroom. There in his words are the ways of the ship and her people – from very stem to very stern. These are the ways as they were, or he thought they were, in the late 1950s. Ways that are ending. The old order changing.

In the autumn of 1957 everyone knew the world was changing faster than since the day it had started to rain over Noah's boatyard, as the Mate once confided. That October the Russians sent a satellite into space – a little silver Sputnik. Technology to be admired. But the rocket that hurled it out there was to be feared. If the rocket was powerful enough to break through the earth's atmosphere into space, then it was powerful enough to carry a nuclear bomb around the world. So, in October 1957, intercontinental warfare was born. They called it MAD: Mutual Assured Destruction. The more hopeful said that the same rockets would take us all to the moon. Maybe to Mars. Pangloss knew a thing or two.

The new ideas to colonise the planets came as a quarter of the globe was thinking about escaping from colonialism. The flag was being lowered on the British Empire. All heady stuff, but not for most parents. They still believed Britain had an empire, still believed British Is Best (or was), just as the Americans still carved into their coins In God We Trust (or trusted). The craft of parenthood was as confusing as ever, maybe more so.

As the wind of change rustled colonialism, the equally fragile covering of authority in the British home was slipping away. Parents who had stumped through the social injustices of the 1930s, the war that followed, the disappointments of the social revolution of the late 1940s and the austerity that seemingly had to be allowed to drift away rather than be swept aside with so-called victory were now losing the one respect they had always relied on: authority.

The connection between loss of the Empire, the running down of national service, and the revolution of television, which brought outside thoughts and wider visions into living rooms, was not a fanciful notion. It existed right enough. It was now harder to say with any authority that the young should have respect for their elders, certainly their betters. What was more, the young were joining a secret society, secret, that is, from their parents. The new anarchy could be found on a mostly crackly 208-metre band. Music that didn't come from the BBC or expensive records. Parents now had rock 'n' roll in the back bedroom. First it had been Haley. Now there was another one – British this time. His name was Tommy Steele. It wasn't, of course. It was Thomas Hicks, but then, when the world's changing, what's in a name? And the connection with the lad? Until he got a guitar and found a place called The Two Eyes Coffee Bar, in Soho, where they'd let him play it, Tom Hicks had been a sailor, a steward in a liner. That made him an even more romantic figure. In these islands, the sailor was still special. Faraway places with strange-sounding names were more than a lyric for pub crooners. Britannia still ruled, or so it was said. A lot of people went to sea in the 1950s. There were a lot of ships, so there were plenty of jobs – even in tramping. That, too, was changing, although not many realised it.

# 2

## LEAVING HOME

Once upon a time, Britain had the biggest fleet in the world. Now the Liberians did. Liberians didn't actually own anything. Companies simply registered their ships there. It was a tax scam. But in that autumn of 1957 there were still more than 400 deep-sea tramps flying the red ensign or the red duster as some liked to call the oblong red bunting with the Union flag in the corner.* There were now more than twenty-three million tons of tramp ships at sea. There never had been such a big fleet. Of that twenty-three million, Britain owned more than four million tons.†

*Royal Fleet Auxiliaries – Board of Trade-owned store and supply ships for the Royal Navy – flew blue ensigns, although they were never called 'blue dusters'. Royal Naval vessels (and members of the Royal Yacht Squadron) fly the white ensign – the flag of St George with the Union flag in the top-left quarter.
† These are 'dead-weight' tons, which is the laden weight of the ship. Sometimes ships use the term 'gross tons': the total enclosed space in a vessel (accommodation, engine room and holds) measured in cubic feet; 100 cubic feet = 1 gross ton.

You could wander about the City of London and find streets of shipping companies. The prosperous ones were in places like Leadenhall Street. In the windows and sturdy brass, oak and mahogany entrance halls were wonderfully detailed models of their fleets. Black-hulled tankers with deep-red bottoms and white superstructures. Brilliant white liners with the cream funnels of P&O. Pale lilac hulls of Union Castle trading down to South Africa. The three black and red funnels of Cunard's *Queen Mary* – still a decade of sailing left in her. But they weren't all massive and smart. Sturdy models of general cargo ships, coasters with all the accommodation aft and, in the older and often darker halls, Victorian sailing ships with thin funnels and giant paddle wheels amidships. Here lay, in properly dusted oblong glass cases, the pride of the nation – its mercantile marine. Here, to a stone building with window boxes, a corps of commissionaires, gate-man and a gold-grilled lift to the fourth floor – the very top in 1957 – came the lad from the Kentish marshes in search of his berth.

## 12 December 1957

There were five of us. We had to sit in this room on a bench. I wanted to get a closer look at the ships in the glass cases. They were all old ones. Cargo. Some of them coal-burners, I think. But there was this woman sitting at a desk by the door. A right rat-face. She was typing away like no one's business and she had these long black bags tied from her wrists to elbows. She really looked horrible. Like the bloke who did my tonsils. I was just going to ask her if I could go toilet, when she looked up and said, No talking! Nobody had said a word. Then this light goes on by the door and she says something. I just stared at her. We all did. It wasn't a word. Just a snarling sound. Then she points her pencil at me and says, You! Next thing, I'm in there and this white-haired bloke with a big pink face is telling me to sit down, really friendly. And he's got spats. Old Mr Mitchell who had the big shop in Erith wore spats. Mum said it was because he was what she called the old school. A gentleman. Dad said that when he was chauffeuring they all wore them. But that was 1930-something, twenty years back. But this chap had them. I could see them sticking under the desk. He said why did I want to go to sea? Dad had said he'd ask that. They always do, he said. Tell them because you want to get to the top and be a Captain of a liner. I remembered those models. These people didn't have liners. So I just said what I thought. I said, because we'd always gone to sea. Which companies, he said. Not actually companies, I told him. Mostly off the Kent coast. Sole. Dabs. Mackerel. Crabs. Fishermen. Then I told him about sailing aboard the barge. That got him going. No engine? No, sir. But a good rig. Gaffer, she is, sir. Gaffer. Sprits'l. She'd tack through ninety and would gybe if you didn't watch her when running and there was no preventer that could handle her if she wanted to gybe and you hadn't watched for it. Sir. Off the sticks at Whitstable it once blew so hard that Mr Bevan the skipper had to put his teeth in his pocket in case they rattled out. He lapped it up. Said I was a proper sailor. Not like those nancy boys in P&O. Next thing he's standing up and shaking my hand. I wasn't quite sure what to do. No one had ever shaken my hand before. I wasn't sure when to let go. When I got outside, the woman said did I have any expenses. What's those? Travelling. That sort of thing. I said I'd come up on the 132 bus. One and three. She opened this little red and black box and gives me half-a-crown. Said that should cover it. So I bought a Mars bar and a bottle of Cherryade.

In those days they would take a lad with four O-levels: English, maths and two others – but proper ones, they'd say. Some boys had been to the sea schools. King Edward VII, the stack of bricks along the Commercial Road in London's East End. Maybe to the Worcester, that black and white hulk moored on the Thames not far from Gravesend. Perhaps to Pangbourne – smarter still. These lads would be taken up by the bigger companies, the likes of P&O, BI, Blue Funnel. There, they called them cadets. Very swept up. Still part of the Raj. The Raj was still there in these ships on the Orient run, with their white officers and cadets and Goanese and Laskari crews. Those apprentices, those cadets, soon knew their chota peg from their dhobi wallah. They soon called for the casab and serang, what our Kentish lad in his tramp steamer would call the storekeeper and bosun. So even in the late 1950s, unlike the inbred democracy of the Royal Navy, the merchant mariners had their own caste system. Why not? It came from Britain's colonial history, which their forefathers and their companies had helped build. A gaudy history of sashes, plumes and white gloves. In The Tramp, the apprentice would have in his locker (but rarely wear) a basic uniform. In the P&O, the cadet would wear not a uniform but a livery. Yes, the Empire lived on at sea.

The rougher end of it was in a basement in The Minories near Tower Bridge. It was to the bowels of the Shipping Federation that father and son went with a list.

## MONDAY 13 JANUARY 1958

Had to go down to this clothing store. They sent Dad a paper. Kit list. There's these two blokes playing some game with dice when we got there. They said it's called Liars. Dad said he'd played Crown and Anchor in the army. One of them said that that was the sort of thing they did in the army. Everyone had a laugh. Nice enough blokes. Smell a bit pongy. One of them had so much Brylcreem on you could see white bits on his ears. And he had it on his eyebrows which were very black and shiny. They seem to know everything. One of them called out the list; the other one got stuff off the shelves and out of boxes. Blue dungarees – one!, shouts one of them. Blue dungarees – one!, shouts the other one. Oilskin, black, large – one! Oilskin, black, large – one! Sou'wester, black – one! Sou'wester, black – one! I told him I was seven and a quarter. Not in a bleedin' gale you're not, sunshine. Get it big and pull it down. Pyjamas, striped, medium – one! I said I supposed to save washing you only wore the bottoms. Just the top, he said. Dad said that was enough of that, but didn't say what that was enough of. We had to have the lot. Blue jersey. Black uniform sox. Seaboots. Seaboot sox – white. Even this white canvas kitbag. Make sure you got your name on it, the one with the thin tash and wavy hair said. They pinch things then? He looked me up and down, then looked at Dad and didn't say anything. Strange bloke. Then we got to the best bit. Uniform. Tunic shirt, white, size fifteen – two! Collars, white, stiff, size fifteen and a half – two! What's your inside leg and waist, laddie, said the big one with the Brylcreem and the silver rings. I didn't know. Dad didn't know. The one with the tash gets out this tape measure. Dad said he'd do the measuring. Then he gets all red and says we could guess. The one with the rings gave me a nice smile and said, Never mind, try these on. Black uniform trousers. I had to go behind this cupboard. They seemed a bit big round the waist. The fat one said they had to be because I would fill out and anyway I was getting braces to go with them. Then he gives me a jacket. Eight gold buttons down the front, four on each side, and little gold things on the collar. Fits really good. Then they gave me the hat. I got it all on and they said have a look in that mirror. It didn't look so good with my grey school shirt, but I really felt great. The one with the tash said which ship was I joining. I told him. They both laughed. Well, he said, you're not going to need that much. I should fetch yourself another set of dungarees if I were you. When we got outside, I said to Dad I thought they were really nice. Blinking shirtlifters, he said. What's that mean? You'll learn, he said. I asked Mum when we got home and she said Dad should button his lip.

So fitted out and with his white canvas kitbag, a blue and grey cardboard suitcase and self-conscious in blue serge (in P&O it would have been doeskin) and cap, the lad begins the most complicated part of his journey – leaving home.

They hadn't wanted him to go. Not because they were close. His father told him. They'd expected him to go to the factory, where his grandfather was a fitter and turner. The grandfather would have put a word in and he'd have started at eight o'clock sharp on the Monday after leaving school. There was a small bag that was rightfully his. In it, a lunch box for his paste sandwiches, a white enamel tea flask, blue overalls. He'd have learned to gather the mild steel sweepings from his grandfather's lathe. Sharp sweepings wet with the milky coolant that stopped the blade glowing as it shaped the fast-revolving end. Plenty of sweeping. Then by the end of the year, a chisel to be made that a craftsman could have shown him how to fashion in ten minutes and with a bit of practice he could have got right in a fortnight. But this was the apprentice time. He'd been expected to serve his time. It would take five years. Cheap labour. Growing up in the shadow of the master craftsman who had made Britain great. That's what they said. He could have learned to sweep up the sticky, sharp swarf and maybe fashion and temper a new tool for industry. A job for life. A Smith's mantel clock at the end of it. There was no brave new world. But he didn't want a boiler suit. His grandfather understood. His father couldn't. He could never know what his mother thought. He might have got close if he'd read her magazines. The headmaster had mentioned university, but his father had said that it was not for them. The factory was best. They hadn't known what to say when he said no.

January came dull. The day to leave was gloomier still by news of an aunt's death. Of course, no one spoke about it. Death was held in awe. Just ten years earlier, the men had gone to war. Some fell. That was different. A telegram. A note on thin paper from an officer. An official form to apply for the medal to be forwarded in a brown cardboard box. How about a nice cup of tea, said the neighbours. They all understood war and not coming back. This wasn't that. His aunt had never been to war, but she'd not hide. A spinster lying in an efficient line of crisply sheeted iron bedsteads, waiting her turn for the end one, the one by the door. No one said. Everyone knew. An aunt eaten away until she screamed to let go, then mercifully doing so was a mystery. A rite of some fearful passage best kept from the lad.

The first knock was the uncle, burly in a brown overcoat, the collar turned up against the wet wind. The look was enough. It was done. But not a word to him. He was old enough to face the ocean, but nothing deeper.

He stood there in his pressed uniform and stiff collar and wanted them to smile, to wish him luck. To admire his polished brass buttons and glossed toecaps of shoes that squeaked. They did their best. They were good, rough men. Good with their hands. They understood fine timber and winds and eddies. None had stood in a drawing room. None had wit for these moments. There was never much to say at any parting, not until the other had gone.

This, the 1950s, was a time when uniforms were commonplace. Young men in this family had polished their buttons, creased their bell-bottoms and Blanco'd their belts for a century. They were no different from any other. It could always have been Aldershot or Catterick, where sneering corporals would have induced him into the world of Britain's conscript army. Maybe Portsmouth. Corporal or killick. It was all the same. Hair cut and double away. They all had to do it. It was not until the 1960s that teenagers were allowed to make their own way into adulthood. Until that decade, all but poets would have short hair. Even pop stars wore white sports coats and pink carnations.

On this day there would be no pink Caddie to take him to his ship. The second knock was the lady down the way to say that her Arthur had sixteen boxes of dabs to shift so he needed the van and couldn't be taking them to the station after all.

So father and son trudged to the small clock tower in the high street to catch the double-decker. Then, with his cardboard case banging against his leg, his kitbag slipping from shoulders not yet broad enough, he climbed the steel and wooden bridge to the up-line for London and Liverpool Street and the magical phrase that would live in his mind for the rest of his life: Liverpool Street to Harwich and the Hook. No more vans of stinking dabs. No more silences.

As he left England and his family to mourn Aunt Eva's passing and perhaps even his going – he'd never really know – the undertakers and embalmers of a quite different persuasion were about their work. For a hundred years, Britain had had an empire. A quarter of the globe was British – even the French knew that. The monarch's head was on more envelopes than any other nation's. A child's stamp album was a magical classroom of history and geography. Australia to Zanzibar. Queen Victoria, him very good man, ran the proud pidgin mantra. The new Elizabethans had not yet understood the complicated chimes of the colonial clock. Macmillan had yet to tell that the wind of change was blowing surely through more than one continent. No zephyr, this was a wind to huff and to puff down the flimsy structures of British colonialism. First Burma and India. Ceylon, a dominion in 1948 until it became the Republic of Sri Lanka twenty-four years later. Within little more than a decade, most of British colonial territories would be handed back to their peoples. Some would not want to leave British rule. Small nations would cling to the apron. Most would shake loose or lose their grip.

When the lad joined The Tramp, she, too, was coming to the end of her time. She had served a grand purpose, and honourably so. She had kept the home fires of commercialism and invisible earnings burning brightly. Perhaps this would be her last circumnavigation of this trade. He did not understand the coincidence. Three deaths were too complicated to explain. Too complicated to take on board.

The instructions were simple: compartment G, Liverpool Street Station, the eight o'clock for Harwich and the Hook. They stood there, three of them. Son, self-conscious. The sergeant, a friend from his father's war. Full of an NCO's humour. A cackle of coarse laughter. Nudging, winking. A conspiracy neither of them knew they were in. Then his father. Still not really understanding. Still not knowing whether he'd failed him. When the doors started slamming, sticking out a hand when he really wanted arms. Neither of them knew how to do that. Instead, from the window he waved. Wrong window. Facing the wrong way. A porter waved back. He'd had no goodbye plan. It wouldn't have been this.

On the night ferry the lad found himself for the first time on a proper ship. The churn of propellers as she manoeuvred from the dock, the vaguely heard clang of the engine room telegraph as she shuddered and gathered her speed from the fairway buoy for the Dutch coast. It was dark, and he stared back at the lights, wondering for just a moment what he was leaving behind. Just a moment.

At the bar in the main saloon, still self-conscious and having fended off three requests from passengers who wanted to know where the lavatories were, he ordered his first proper drink. He'd heard an uncle talk about whisky macs. Didn't know what they were, but they sounded pretty grown up. So breaking into the precious £5 note his father had given him during their gruff goodbye, he ordered one. He had a second one and then thankfully headed for his pillow, already unsteady and still not knowing what a whisky mac was although somehow he thought it Christmassy.

The next morning, his gear together, he trod carefully down the long ferry gangway. For a moment he stood as others went on. Tall grey cranes. Brown goods waggons waiting for the first bales to swing ashore. Tugs and coasters busily making room for the blue-hulled ocean-goers. Round- and ruddy-faced dockers, most with caps, most with black clogs. A smell of something he would never understand but would always be there. He hefted his kitbag, picked up his case and headed along the wet wharf. His shoes had stopped squeaking. The lad had left England.

From the quay he read her painted stern. Black, hard hull and shiny white name. He said it quietly to himself. Already proud, then feeling the dark eyes peering from the top of the gangway, he stepped steadily along the wharf, his kitbag still slipping from his narrow shoulders. Not enough string around his cheap bulging suitcase. Trying not to hurry, trying not to feel excited, trying not to feel frightened, trying not to look so new.

The Tramp was just as he had seen her two years before in the Royal Docks. Nothing special. Now here she was in Amsterdam. The cranes all ready, at eight o'clock in the morning, unloading buff-brown bales from her five holds. As he started to climb the white-slatted and chained gangway up to the main deck, he stumbled with his cardboard suitcase and canvas kitbag. He could feel the stares of the Dutch dockers and the Chinese quartermaster at the top of the gangway and felt no comfort in his grandfather's goodbye.

'You'll be coming back a man. Mind you do it well.'

## 28 JANUARY 1958, AMSTERDAM

She really feels big and she feels hard; there are no soft bits anywhere. Everything is steel. The decks are all red and the superstructure is white. The Captain and all the officers live in the superstructure where the bridge is. I'm down with the other apprentice, the engineers and some others, who I don't know what they do, in the middle bit, which is under the funnel. The funnel is huge. Red then a white and red band then a black top. I suppose that's to hide all the soot marks when she smokes. I'm sharing a cabin. His name's Ainslie and this is his second trip and he says his last. I've got the top bunk which apparently is given to the most junior. That doesn't seem very bright to me, though I haven't said so. Every time you get up into the top bunk you have to put your foot on the bottom bunk. I'd have thought anybody would have spotted that. The other thing is that if anybody comes in they always sit on the bottom bunk to chat. Hope I don't get promoted.

A deck apprentice signed indentures just as in any other trade. He was bound to the shipping company for four years. During that time the company could more or less do what it would with him. In tramp ships, the voyages were usually very long. It was common for a crew to be away for eighteen months, sometimes two years. Everyone had to sign what were known as articles. Articles were simply the terms of contract of employment. That contract lasted two years. For the sailor there was a get-out clause, and it existed between the port of Brest in France and Kiel in northern Germany. It meant that if a ship left, say, Southampton, the sailor would have to stay on board, because of the articles he had signed, for a full two years. However, if the vessel returned to any European port between Brest and Kiel, then the sailor could demand to be sent home. In fact, companies rarely faced demands because it was always a good opportunity to change over a whole crew and sign new articles.

For the apprentice boy, there was none of the advantage of being on two-year articles because he was bound by the four-year indentures. Moreover, there were certain ways of keeping him at sea and away from the United Kingdom for longer than the rest of the crew. For example, if a ship put into Genoa, a crafty company, knowing that she was then heading to the Far East for another two years, might take that opportunity to change the crew, because the travel between Genoa and London would be reasonably cheap, and then get the new crew to sign on for another two years. So it was quite possible for an apprentice to go away and not get home for more than three years.

He hadn't known that when he'd signed his indentures in that London office. Didn't know it now as he signed his name, his mark, in the tall, thin log lying on the blue felt cloth in the ship's saloon. If he had known, he wouldn't have cared. This was home. Seven thousand or so gross tons, 425 feet long, 56-foot beam and about 27-foot draught, depending on tropical, summer or winter loadings. She carried a master, seven British mates and engineers, a wireless operator and two, sometimes three, apprentice boys. Aft, in the depths of the stern, with the grinding and rumble of the five-bladed propeller, lived twenty-seven Hong Kong Chinese deckhands, donkeymen, stokers and greasers. The stewards and carpenter lived amidships.

## 30 JANUARY 1958, ON BOARD

Ainslie took me for what he calls the half-a-crown tour. He's been on board for eighteen months and loathes it. I asked him why. He didn't say anything, just looked at me as if I'm simple. Odd bloke. Really tall and skinny and he looks very grumpy.

She's a long ship with a black hull and white superstructure in three blocks. The fo'c's'le is raised with a double steam windlass. Then on the main for'd deck, two long hatches with tarpaulin covers with wooden wedges holding them tight. Just big versions of the sailing barge. When I said this, Ainslie said was I a cockney. I said no. Cockneys were from East London and were supposed to be born within the sound of the bells of Bow Church. He said I seemed to know a lot about it so I must be one. Strange bloke.

The for'd accommodation is on three decks. The main deck is the smoke room, saloon (which Ainslie says we're not allowed in, only officers) and the three Mates' cabins, the chief steward's plus the pantry, and on the starboard side the stairs up to the Captain's accommodation and then up to the bridge. The Captain has the whole of the first deck to himself plus the owner's cabin which

Ainslie says is just a small one for a passenger, although he'd never seen any in his eighteen months. We're not allowed up there. I asked Ainslie what would happen if there were a hurricane or something. Wouldn't it be safer to go up to the bridge on the inside through the Captain's flat? He shrugged. Said if I wanted to try it that was fine by him but the Old Man would have me ashore like a flash of pig-shit. The upper deck is the bridge, chartroom and wireless room plus a cabin for the wireless operator who everyone calls the Sparks. Behind all this on deck is number three hatch and then the 'midships accommodation, funnel and boat deck. Then two more hatches and the after-mast. Right aft is the poop, where we carry the spare propeller and emergency steering wheel. Below decks is crew accommodation. It's really clean but it's got a funny smell. Ainslie says it's a Chinese smell. He says everyone smells different. According to him, they think we smell of butter. I said, How do you know? He said, Everyone knows. I didn't.

So this is the lad's new village. Far removed from the Kentish tile-hung community with his dad on a push-bike, his lunch in a gas-mask bag. His mother hanging out the washing but drying their underwear in the bathroom. His auntie next door for ever chattering to her blue budgie called Billie. His pipe-smoking godfather for ever in his workshop making sawdust. Mr Derrett and Mr Dorman weighing out quarter-pounds of lemon sherbets, marking up the *Daily Herald*, the *News Chronicle*, *The Dispatch* and *Kentish Times* for his early-morning round. Thelma behind the till ordering a purl one, drop one knitting pattern for Miss Hammond, who ran her father's bakery. Dodging the hurled stones and fist-shaking of old Mr Marshall as he scrumped his apples. Choir practice Friday nights. Maybe

1s. 6d. for a Saturday wedding and being told off by Mr Warren, the choirmaster, when his voice cracked on the second verse of 'There Is a Green Hill Far Away'. His mother crying, his father thinking it was just a bum note, then embarrassed. Most of all, long moments gazing across the marshes to the great liners, tramps and colliers on their ways to and from the docks and wharves along the Thames. This now was real. So, too, was the new language – not the Cantonese of the deckhands and donkeymen but the centuries-old seamen's dialect.

In his Thames sailing barge he'd already learned the sign language and codes of the sailorman. As other lads of his age knew about inside rights, halfbacks, googlies and chinamen, drop handlebars, 78s and EPs, so he was at home with bowsprits, gaffs, mains'ls and mizzens, port and starboard, stem and starn, head ropes and stern ropes, springs and warps.

He knew the sailors' tongue. Port was left, starboard was right. For'd was forward, at the sharp end, the bow. Aft was the back, the stern. Abaft was behind, behind anything. The fo'c's'le, the raised deck of the bow with its anchor windlass. The poop, the raised deck at the stern. Amidships, the middle of the ship and abeam, at ninety degrees to the ship either on the starboard side or the port side. So when you were facing the front – for'd – something that was abaft the starboard beam was sort of over your right shoulder. The kitchen was the galley, the dining room the saloon, the sitting room the smoke room, the lavatory the heads. And everyone's own room was a cabin. No bedrooms. Cabins. Beds were bunks. Wardrobes, lockers. The ceiling in his cabin was not a ceiling but a deckhead. The walls were not walls but bulkheads. The windows were not windows but scuttles. Only the holes themselves were portholes, which were never called portholes, only ports. And he had no floor in his cabin. It was a sole, and when he got outside it was no longer the sole but the deck.

Naturally. The lad had to learn that when he climbed the mast he was going aloft. When he came down he was going below. There were no stairs, only ladders and companionways. He never, never went downstairs. Only below. Then, of course, there was the monkey island, that windswept platform on top of the bridge and wheelhouse, with its signal mast, emergency steering wheel and a big wooden chest, the fog locker, of lanterns and navigation shapes. It was, too, where the Third Mate worked on his tan.

## 31 JANUARY 1958

She's big, but not as big as a lot of ships. Tankers are bigger. She's about 7,000 tons, although I'm not sure what that means. I've got my Ian Allen books of ships with me and there's a picture of the Blue Star boat, the *Scottish Star*, and she's just under 10,000 tons, although she doesn't look any bigger. Our ship's 425 feet long. It feels great. Just walking along the deck is great. It makes a strong sound. Everything you see is there for a proper reason. Nothing fancy. The steam pipes are there to drive the winches, which means you don't need cranes from shoreside. The big steel disc things that you clamp over the ports in storms mean you don't have to rely on good weather. There are watertight doors, ventilators about as big as small elephants, grabrails as thick as my wrist, bollards for tying on ropes that are as thick as small tree trunks. Each hatch board is twice as long as our dining table and the hatch covers [tarpaulins] are as big as our back garden – maybe bigger. When you go up the for'd ladder, you feel you're going up to something that's going to do something. I went up there this morning and although it's all quiet at the moment it felt strong and waiting. This may sound daft, but I know what I mean. The fo'c's'le deck is red. Right in the middle is the windlass. It's black and huge with big drums on either side. So when the time comes to haul in the ropes, they'll go round the drums and then the sailors will tail them off in big loops. I've seen them do it in the Vic and KG5.* The whole thing's driven by steam and it looks really terrific when it starts hissing and the winchman spins the steam handle. Then there are two giant chains coming up through the decks through holes which I think are called spurling pipes. These are the anchor chains. We haven't got the anchors out. Don't need to alongside, but I can't wait until we're somewhere we can anchor. We had to do it on the barge. Great noise and you have to know what the sea bottom is like. No good anchoring on rocky bottoms. Deep sand is best, I think Frank Bevan said.

I've only been here a couple of days, but I know one thing for sure: a ship isn't meant to be in port. She's supposed to be at sea.

*The Royal Victoria and King George v Docks at Woolwich.

# 3

## A GOOD RUN ASHORE

This was the strangest environment. People worked together during the day, ate together, laughed together and argued together. They did that in the factory in Erith. But then the hooter sent them home. In the tramp, no one went home. They took their differences to their cabins, but they were only a bulkhead apart. So the cabin was special. It was a sanctuary. Few casual callers. A place where a letter might be left open. Yet a door was rarely closed at sea. A curtain pulled across. Nothing sturdier. Still, going to someone else's cabin demanded a certain protocol. Courtesies were observed. Always knock, even when the curtain was drawn. Wait for 'come in'. A visitor might get a glass for his beer but he'd never dream of sitting anywhere but the long leatherette bench which was grandly called a settee. He'd never plonk down in the desk chair. That would be like trying to take Communion from the wrong side of the rail. Yet for all that, settling in wasn't difficult.

The protocols were obvious because so, too, was the pecking order. Ten officers and two deck apprentices didn't take much working out. The Captain was really called the Master and privately the Old Man. The Mate – and only the Mate – would refer to him as Father. The Captain, the Master, Father was never spoken to unless he spoke first. No one other than the Chief Engineer ever tapped at the Master's door for a casual chat. Not even the Mate. The Mate was both glove and punchbag. He ran the ship on behalf of the Master and rolled with brickbats and let none reach the Master. The Mate's authority was the hardest to maintain. Stern, fair, chummy, distant and always to blame. Get it wrong and the trip was unhappy. Get it right and the next job as Master could be his. The Second Mate had nothing to do with you unless you were his apprentice on the twelve to four o'clock watch. He looked after the charts, the gyrocompass and himself. The Third Mate was easy-going, close to your age and was certainly young enough and inexperienced enough for the Master to wonder if he were any good and the Mate to assume that he wasn't. Talking to engineers was like talking to in-laws – officially part of the ship's family, but a different breed. All this took time to work out for the lad. But he would.

## 31 JANUARY 1958

I'm not yet sure who speaks and who doesn't. The Mate is quite fierce. He's not as tall as me but he's very round and he's got an enormous beard. And he's Irish. When he speaks he makes gurgling sounds at the back of his throat. It's like he had a bit of his whiskers caught down there. The Second Mate just stared at me when Ainslie said who I was. Then he nodded. Then he said was I keen on crosswords. I said I didn't know. I'd never done

one. He just walked away. The chief steward's Chinese and has a big smile. Ainslie says we have to keep in with him. Because he's got the food? No. Because he's the biggest sneak on the sodding ship and he'll tell on you if he feels like it. Ainslie says I'll soon get to know everyone. He says there was no need to speak to the engineers unless you wanted to. He says you'll soon know who they are. They always wipe their hand on their trousers before they shake hands – even when they're perfectly clean. Habit, he said. Don't take any notice. They're not like us. I said, My granddad's an engineer. He said, You'll know what I mean then.

The ship was a happy ship, a good feeder or a bastard of a ship. Ask any sailor, and that would be more or less what he'd say. Who called the cook a bastard, the Mate wanted to know. Who called the bastard a cook, someone replied. They said it every trip. A ritual of insult and belonging. You belonged when you knew all the insults and when to make them. The Tramp had a reputation as a happy ship, but then it was also true that a sailor's last ship was always the best ship. There was something solid about her. Strong rivets, their heads bigger than a silver half-crown piece. Red steel deckplates that sounded hard and sure beneath the scuff of boots and dragged chain. Black and rusting scuppers that were thick enough to take another rat-a-tat-tat of chipping hammers. Bollards and bits that would never give beneath the stress of huge hawsers. Old mahogany and teak in the saloon and smoke room. Heavy dark blue curtains to set off the polished brass scuttles. The silent icon of the whole vessel, the ship's wheel, with gleaming, varnished spokes each longer than the quartermaster's arm. Brass studs in the 'north' spoke that let you know when the wheel was centred. 'Wheel amidships, sir,' sang out the quartermaster. All very simple. All very reliable. Everything to hand. No ornaments. Into this tough old tramp the seamen fitted easily and, on a good day, with each other. Most were good days. They soon tested each other and themselves. Like that first run ashore – the sailors' night out.

You could tell a sailor in the 1950s. Mostly he was the smartest, most scrubbed in the bar. No images of blue jerseys and white seaboot socks. In The Tramp, there'd be much sprucing. The four Ss, the Mate called it in a rare lapse into the crudeness he would normally leave to others: shit, shave, shower and shampoo. Then slick, some even elegant, down the gangway in shined shoes and pressed Hong Kong suit. Every run ashore was a Saturday night out. For a young lad, ashore for the first time, it could be a memorable experience.

## 1 FEBRUARY 1958

I don't think I've got off to a good start. I feel ill. It happened two days ago. Nearly two nights now. I'd signed on. We all had. Ainslie says did I fancy a run ashore? Everyone was going and I had to get me civvies on. I haven't got any. You little turd, he said. I don't think he means it. It's just the way he speaks. I thought you went ashore in uniform. Think you're on a sodding battle-ship, he said. He told the Mate I hadn't got any civvies. They never told me on the list, I said. The Mate's a nice bloke. He told me to get myself ashore and see if I could find a shop for a jacket and a pair of kecks. I told Ainslie. What's kecks? Trousers. Why can't he say trousers? Why can't you sodding do as you're told and get ashore? I told him I hadn't got any money. Back to the Mate and he fixed it for me.

I've never bought any clothes before. Mum's always done that. I wasn't sure where to go. These Dutch blokes all speak English. I asked the one on the dock gate if he knew where there was a

Co-op. He looked a bit dim. Then someone from the agent's office came by and said the best think to do was to go to something called the Centrum (I think). I said did they sell jackets and how much did he think they were? He said it was the centre of town and I could buy anything I liked there. I was hoping he'd give me a lift, but he just pointed and so I had to walk because I wasn't sure how much money I'd need. It took ages. This place is huge. I think it's called Rotterdam, or it may be the other one, Amsterdam. I wonder what 'dam' means? I don't expect it's as big as London. It can't be that big if it hasn't got a Co-op. Even Erith's got a Co-op. It took me a couple of hours to find the shops. I got a blue corduroy jacket for thirty guilders. I'm not sure how much that is. The trousers were fourteen. Then I couldn't find my way back. It was dark when I eventually found the rotten ship. Ainslie was going barmy. Said I'd been skiving and why had I got this funny jacket? Said I looked like a sodding poofter in it. I suppose it is a funny blue. It looked all right in the shop. It doesn't now. Bit bright. As Mum would say, it shows the dirt. I said it was the same colour as Erith & Belvedere play in, that's why they call them the blues. Thanks for that gem, said Ainslie. He supports Preston North End. He would. I said I'd seen Tom Finney. I thought that was being friendly. Ainslie said, I bet Finney never saw you, and then told me to be ready by seven-thirty or the Mate'd have my guts for garters. I wonder if the Mate wears garters?

When they went ashore, they all wore suits or blazers. This was the 1950s. A crocodile of clerks and drummers descending in seniority down the rickety ship's gangway. Some, like the Mate and the Second Engineer, wore trilby hats. The Second had bought his in Cape Town.

Light brown felt, with an antelope-fur band. He claimed that when he wore it in London, people thought he might be a diamond millionaire. No one bothered to ask the Second who such gullible people might be. But it was the 1950s and, anyway, no one asked the Second Engineer very much. He was a lonely figure. Usually ashore by himself. Always returning sadder than when he went. Sometimes beaten up. Often penniless. Ever philosophical. Never grim in his discontent. There were four, sometimes five engineers. On board they were called the Chief – who regarded himself on a par with the Captain – the Second, the Third and the Fourth and, occasionally, the Fifth. Unlike deck officers, engineers were rarely given their full titles except in the ship's papers or on their cabin doors. So when someone referred to the Second, everyone knew he was talking about the Second Engineer and not the Second Mate. The Chief Officer was called The Mate. Next to him on the port side lived the Second Mate. On the starboard side, between the smoke room and the chief steward, was the Third Mate's cabin.

The first run ashore was the getting-to-know-you night. Each had found his place and his role aboard the ship. Engineers had looked over the three great steam reciprocators. They'd tapped and run up the donkey engine. Checked the boiler room. Fuel lines and bunkers. The Mate had talked routine with the Master and bosun. The Second Mate had checked the charts and the dates they were last corrected in thin-nibbed mauve ink. The Third Mate had looked over the lifeboats and the medicine chest. The deck apprentices had kept out of the way and discussed among themselves what sort of bastard was the Mate. All this done, here was the first time to relax.

Mates and engineers sitting at a round table in a bar of toffee Dutch pipe tobacco and bottles of Oranjeboom. A time for each to weigh the others. Not quite strangers. They all knew someone and all knew someone who knew someone. A few had sailed with the company for years. Been an engineer in this and that ship. A Mate on that or this bridge. With this old bastard Chief and that old bastard skipper. So, like most sailors who keep their own counsel, they had plenty to say and a few said it. Personalities fell into place and pecking order. During the long voyage ahead, anxieties and annoyances would slip out, but that night around the big table, round after round of Oranjeboom would be drunk, the empties stacked in front of them like some bottling plant waiting to start the morning shift. Here basic truths about the band of brothers would be established.

The Mate, short, bearded with a large, round, hard stomach. The Second Mate, quick and quiet witted, dark eyed and shadowed jaw no razor would lighten. The Third Mate, tall, elegant, very young, promoted from the apprentices' cabin. Primrose socks and narrow suede shoes. The Second, anxious, grey-stubbled dome, watery blue eyes flickering across his beer glass rim at the young lad. The Third, kind face and soft Scottish lilt, with a locker of funny jokes – none to make his auntie in Montrose blush. The Fourth, once an engineer, then a policeman, now once more an engineer. Stern-faced, humour-less, still on duty. The other apprentice, from the north country, always fingering his nose, the aggressiveness of a confident orphan, even in the company of the elders. The lad, watching and listening. Uncertain.

## 2 FEBRUARY 1958

I feel ill. I'm not sure what happened. First the Mate put some money in the middle of the table. Everyone else did the same. I didn't have much. But the apprentices only have to put in a little.

Apparently that's the rule, according to the Third Engineer. When that was finished, they did it again. Then it just went on. All this beer. Nothing like this happens at home. At least I don't think so. I've never been in a pub. Only the garden. They just keep on drinking. Then some Dutch blokes came over and it all started again. I remember wondering where they kept all these bottles. Hundreds of them. I think I was OK until I got outside. I remember falling over and then someone sort of carrying me. Ainslie says the tricky bit was getting me back on board. The gangway wasn't there. Well it was, but the Chinkie quartermaster had gone off for a smoke and pulled it up, then it had jammed and he couldn't get it down, so he threw the pilot ladder over the side. That meant going up the side of the ship on this silly little rope thing with a few bits of wooden struts. Ainslie says they got me nearly to the top then, according to him, I said I was going to be sick and tried to jump off. We're almost light ship [empty] and it had to be sixty feet down to the dock. Ainslie said as far as he was concerned he'd have let me and that he can already see that I'm a tossing nuisance. Apparently, it was the Third Engineer who was coming up behind me who managed to get hold of me. The quartermaster sent a line down and the Third tied it round my waist. Somehow. I don't remember what happened then until they got me stripped off. This was the worst bit. They threw me in the shower and turned the cold on really hard. I remember that I implored them to turn it off. That was really strange. I'm not sure what 'implore' means. I must have read it in a book somewhere. I heard Ainslie saying, I'll give him implore. Then he said, Stick a broom handle up his bum; that would teach him a lesson. I think he would have done, but then something hit me across the back and I fell over again and I don't remember a thing until Ainslie was shaking me at seven in the morning and telling me that I was a lazy turd and did I think I was on my daddy's yacht and it was time to turn to and the Mate wanted the tarpaulins off the for'd hatches before the wharfies started at eight. I've got a big bandage on my head and the pillow's all bloody. Ainslie says I'll have to pay for it and the Third Engineer shouldn't have bothered.

The world felt grim. It kept moving just when he'd got it in sight. The bitter Dutch morning should have been magic to his young eyes and ears. The grinding of the winches and rumbling cranes. The crashing of the silver hatch beams as they were hoisted clear for unloading the rest of the cargo. Giant hooks plundering fiercely the deep hold like some arcade amusement dipping for a pennyworth of sugared liquorice. The sticky sweetness of hemp and hessian as bale after bale of Havana sugar was hauled and swung higher and higher until they cleared the coamings then swung outboard of the ship's rails and into the railway trucks loitering on the dockside below. The wind off the river iced the lungs. Dripping red nose ends were wiped on the backs of canvas gauntlets. Blue-dungareed dockers slipped cold steel hooks into the eyes of worn strops and steadied bales as they raised an arm with that universal spiralling signal for the crane-man to hoist away. Everywhere was the smell of going foreign for the first time. A waft of ground coffee. The caramel smoke from stubby meerschaums. Strange white spirit taken in nips in the dockside café. The thud and shuffle of wooden clogs on wharf and decks. And the language. Strange Dutch spoken through wetted gums and cavernous palates. This magic absorbed, like the drink the night before, in a blur. Instead, an apprentice boy at each end, the tarpaulin had to be dragged back across the broad hatch top. A stiff green counterpane to be rolled and folded out of harm's and dockers' ways. Long, heavy metal-ended hatch boards to be hefted, dropped and stacked where none could trip over them and disappear noisily and dreadfully down the gaping hold. Awkward, shin-barking work for a lad who didn't know how on a cold river morning without breakfast but with his first hangover. Never again, he had retched into the slippery basin. Not the first to say so. Not the last time he would say so.

## 2 FEBRUARY 1958

I saw the Third Engineer this morning and said thank you. Maybe he saved my life. He just smiled and said next time perhaps I should take more water with it. He's Scotch. I heard the Captain asking the Mate why I had a plaster on my head. The Mate said I slipped in the shower. I suppose that's right.

The Mate was the man the Master always asked. About anything. So it was the Mate who was supposed to know everything, especially the answer to the catch-all question, 'Everything all right, mister?' Everything meant everything other than the state of the engines. Was the running gear working? Were the stores aboard and stowed? Were chart corrections done? Had the cabins been 'dosed' for cockroaches? Was the Third Mate shaping up? Did the cargo stow properly? Was she ready for sea? The iodine-stained plaster on the lad's forehead really wasn't important. Nice enough to enquire? No. Just to make sure the new deck apprentice wasn't a troublemaker. The ship was ready for sea. It was time to go.

The P-flag, a white one with a dark blue border, was hoisted to the starboard spreader of the signal mast. P. The international code flag for 'vessel about to put to sea'. Alongside it, on another halyard, the blue and yellow vertical-striped G-flag. 'I require a pilot'. That's it. Time to be gone.

●

# 4

## PUTTING TO SEA

In his engineless Thames sailing barge, especially in the wind, leaving port was often a tricky and always a highly skilled manoeuvre. Where was the wind? Pushing the vessel on to the wharf? Pushing her off? Where was the tide? Which way was it running? Would it push the bow off the wharf or swing the stern in the wrong direction? Which way was the current running when she got midstream? Was the wind blowing one way and the tide flowing the other? When there is just a skipper and his deckhand to let go the head and stern ropes, hold her on the long spring running the length of the vessel and then, as her head comes off, slip her at just the right moment with the deep-tan sails hoisted, the main scandalised so she won't sail until the topping lift is dropped and she sets, then backed and at the right moment . . . well, yes, all of that. Years of skill and precious instinct were required. The barge he understood. Aboard The Tramp, the new apprentice boy could only watch and marvel when leaving the wharf at Amsterdam.

The first difference was the number of people. The Second Mate, in his white cap as jaunty and crumpled as a Spitfire pilot's, was at the stern with seven deckhands and the senior apprentice. For'd, high on the fo'c's'le, was the Mate, the Chief Officer, with another seven and the casab on the steam windlass. Up on the bridge the Master, the Third Mate standing by the brass-cased engine room telegraph, the quartermaster on the wheel, the Dutch pilot who, the Master hoped, really did know these waters like the back of his hand, and in the corner of the wheelhouse the junior apprentice recording it all in the small bridge book. Then there was the machinery. Big steam windlasses to clatter in the great ropes. The steam reciprocating engines down below to ease the power for'd or astern. Standing off with a line to the ship's bow, a tug ready to pull her head into the stream.

The Tramp was secured with huge ropes. Long lines they called springs ran from the bows back to a bollard ashore somewhere nearly the length of the ship; another ran from the stern to another shoreside bollard, this one close to the ship's bow. The head rope ran from the fo'c's'le to yet another bollard well ahead, and a similar rope ran from the stern to a point thirty feet ashore and astern.

When the time came for all this paraphernalia of mooring and unmooring to break into life, the order came from the bridge. Stand-by engines. The two brass handles on the telegraph were eased forward to 1 o'clock. From deep below, the engine room telegraph answered with a clanking of bells as the engineer on watch repeated the signal. Stand-by engines. All was ready. Now was the time for the umbilical to be broken. Let go the springs – the long ropes that ran fore and aft that stopped the ship surging for'd or astern. The ropes were slackened in a huge dip from bow and stern until the men on the dock could slip their looped ends away from the bollards. Then with much hissing and clanking the winchmen aboard The Tramp spun the L-shaped steam handles. The deckhands took a turn about the great drums as the hawsers slipped from the dock with huge splashes into the harbour and were pulled high up the sheer black steel-riveted sides and coiled on to the ship's deck.

The pilot, chewing on his yellow clay pipe, advised it time to go, and the command came from the Captain, Let go fore and aft. The apprentice boy spoke quietly, with no great confidence at this, his first direct action aboard, into the grey bridge telephone. It connected to one on the poop, manned by the senior apprentice. Let go aft. Let go aft, came the reply, and then without waiting for acknowledgement the senior apprentice yelled down to the after deck and the Second Mate: Let go aft, sir!

On the wing of the bridge the Third Mate called the order for'd and the head and stern ropes were hauled in as quickly as the winches and deckhands could gather them. The tug picked up the tension on the bow hawser. As she came free, the pilot, in a quiet aside, ordered: Slow ahead. At the same time the poop telephone went. All gone aft. All gone aft, sir, the apprentice repeated, not quite sure whether he should be telling the pilot, the Third Mate or the Captain. The Third Mate relayed the news to the wing of the bridge where the Captain and the pilot now stood, watching her clear the side and pull into the main stream. Sedately as an old proud swan she gathered her own speed, and the taut wire to the tug was slipped and the pilot ordered: Starboard five degrees, wheel amidships, half ahead. The Tramp and the lad from the Kentish marshes were on their way to the Orient.

## 3 FEBRUARY 1958

You have to watch her move because it's not like the barge; you don't feel her move. When the barge shifts, even in the river, I can feel the hull give a bit of roll. Frank Bevan says she does it just to let you know she's there. When she's cast off, the barge is different from when she's alongside, even if she's caught in a wash. I sometimes can feel my feet touching the deck. That's sounds potty. It's not. If I walk down the street, I don't think about my feet on the pavement. When I'm on deck in the barge, my feet feel different. Sort of alive. I suppose it's because the decks move and the pavement doesn't. In this ship it's different. The engines make a sort of rumbling noise and everyone's doing something, but there's no sense of movement. I bet when we get into deep sea it'll be different. There's a bit of a chop in the river and estuary, but that doesn't do anything to her. Couldn't really. She's 7,000 tons of steel. I can't quite understand how anything so heavy can float. I know it's all to do with air spaces and centres of gravity and things (I think), but it's still a bit of a puzzle. Seven thousand tons is enormous. I was thinking how heavy Uncle Heron's sacks of spuds are. Each one is fifty-six pounds. That's just half a hundredweight. If you put it at the wrong angle in the barrow the whole thing tips up. Half a hundredweight. So there are forty sacks of his spuds in a ton. Imagine 7,000 tons: that's 280,000 sacks. How can it float? It's not like a barge. She's wood. Wood floats.

One of the first tasks out of port was to swing the compass – the most important instrument on board. It told the navigator in which direction the ship was heading – or pretty close to it. The Tramp was no smart craft down by the head with technology. In the 1950s there wasn't much anyway. Navigation satellites were a quarter of a century away. A few ships had something called Decca or another something called Loran. They were more or less the same system run by different organisations. Loran or Decca were boxes that received signals from shore beacons. The signals joined together and produced a reasonably accurate latitude and longitude.

Nothing was that accurate in those days and, anyway, a position on the chart was usually marked with a pencil thick enough to make pinpoint accuracy unlikely. But it was nice to know that if you were bound for Charleston then you weren't heading for Jacksonville.

The nearest The Tramp got to technology was something called RDF: Radio Direction Finder. Very simply, there was a grey metal box the size of a television screen with a big black watch-face dial marked with the circle of a compass and its 360 degrees. A long-wave radio beam was picked up from shore stations, quite often lighthouses. They came to the ship, one at a time, in the form of a single signal. It was easy to identify because the ship knew the frequency. The operator was usually the radio officer because it was in the radio shack. It was his. He would listen to the identification signal from the shore station, so he knew which one he was tracking. Then he would hear the signal itself – which lasted for about eight seconds. The trick was to tune the ship's aerial not to get the sound at its loudest but at its lowest, because that meant the aerial must be pointing directly at the source of the beam. So the operator would tune the dial around the compass degrees until the tone almost disappeared. He read off the bearing, the point on the compass where the tone disappeared. He then knew that his ship was somewhere along that line. It gave him direction, and if he knew where he was along the line then he knew where he was – sort of. If he did it with other beams, then he could get quite a good idea of the ship's position. The problem was that the RDF beams couldn't be picked up anywhere. Anyway, no sailor trusted technology that much. Not in those days.

One day, technology would take over until sailors didn't have to know a single thing about navigation other than tides. Even then, a big ship simply wound up the engine to deal with tides and sailed along dredged channels to deal with the likes of neaps and springs. By the 1990s even yachtsmen would have hand-held technology that could position them within yards, or by that time metres. But not in the late 1950s.

There was radar, of course, but not on The Tramp. An aid to navigation, said the sailors. An aid to collision, said head office. The best lookout is the Mark I Eyeball. Nonsense, of course, but the accountant believed it, so that made it true – even when they hit a tanker in fog in the Strait of Gibraltar. The lad was on the fo'c's'le that night, so he had his own views. All of that still to come. For the moment, he was learning why the ship was going round in a circle instead of pressing on down the Channel for Biscay, the Med and who knew where after that.

Everyone knows a compass needle points to the north. Well, it doesn't, but it's close. Take a magnet and move it about in front of a compass and the needle follows it. That's what happens to a ship's compass. Its needle is magnetised and it points at the huge mass of ore near the North Pole. This is called Magnetic North. (The Antarctic is all ice, which is why a compass doesn't point south.) Steering a ship by compass means that the helmsman has to know where north is. After all, if he's told to steer north-east, that is forty-five degrees, the first question is: forty-five degrees starting from where? In other words, where's the top of the circle? If the helmsman is just two degrees out and the ship's only going ten miles, then it doesn't much matter. But it's 3,000 and more miles across the Atlantic. That two degrees of error opens into a huge arc of hundreds of miles at the other end of the voyage. First stop Charleston. Should have been Jacksonville.

So by pointing the ship at something you knew was fixed – like a landmark – you could easily see if the compass was pointing to the left or right of where it should be. Why wouldn't it?

It's kitchen-table science. Put a steel carving knife on the table near the compass and the compass needle will wander. Everyone knows that. So does the navigator, especially in a steel ship, with steel boilers, steel engines, derricks, winches and miles of wiring and a couple of carving knives in the galley to boot. And each time the ship changes direction, the effect of all that metal is different. If the ship is pointing west, the iron may set the compass three degrees east off course. If she's heading south-west, it could be four degrees or perhaps nothing at all. And just as every kitchen-table experiment is different, so is each ship. What's more, each ship is likely to change when, for example, the carving knife is moved. Engine repairs, a boiler survey, wiring changes, even cargo (imagine the effects of scrap metal) can alter the metallic influences on the compass.

The only way to check what the deviation – which is what this is called – is doing to the compass is to find a clear area of water close to land, line the compass on a fixed point ashore, whose position you therefore know exactly and what its true bearing should be, and then turn your ship through 360 degrees, noting all the time the compass bearing. Having done this, it is a laborious but simple task to work out the deviation. If the object is bearing due west, that is 270 degrees, but should, according to the chart, be 272 degrees, then the navigator knows that the deviation in the ship on that course (270 degrees) is two degrees, and when he sails for Charleston he can adjust his course accordingly. This circling manoeuvre is known as swinging the compass; it is swung through 360 degrees so that the navigator can make his deviation chart, usually a wiggly line which doesn't look much but, in the technically naked Tramp, was important. They had a gyrocompass on board which gave them a true heading, but what if that went wrong? Swinging the compass was essential.

It was all a bit much for the lad to take in. He went to his textbook. The language was terse, unfriendly. Written by people who didn't know how to tell and, even if they had known, probably wouldn't have done. Much better to remain one-eyed and on the throne. For the moment the lad was thrown into a language and routine not much different from the apprentices of his great-uncle's time in square-rigged brigs and barques.

## 4 FEBRUARY 1958, ENGLISH CHANNEL

The Mate asked me if I had a sextant. I told him I'd got my Great-Uncle Elliot's. He laughed and said, Is it any good? Good enough to get Great-Uncle Elliot round Cape Horn, I said. Really, he said. More than once, I said. Thought it was worth telling him. Perhaps not. He lit a cigarette and wandered off to the other side of the bridge. I don't think he believed me. I'm not even sure it's true. Maybe I shan't mention that again.

## 7 FEBRUARY 1958

We can still get the BBC on Ainslie's radio. There's been a real disaster. A load of the Manchester United team have been killed. Ainslie says the plane crashed or something in snow in Germany. He also says that Frank Swift has been killed. Him and Sam Bartram must be the greatest goalkeepers in the world. I saw Bartram at Charlton. I've got a signed picture of Swift. How can this happen? The weather out here is awful and I'm already feeling seasick, but I feel safer in these waves than on an aeroplane. I think they're dangerous. How can all that metal stay up there? Ships are safer.

Safer, but still vulnerable to indignity. It would look so fine. The black, strong steel hull. White superstructure not yet running with rust streaks. The funnel with its hoops of bright red, black and white. The dark blue, then black and spumy seas sending silver sprays across the fo'c's'le. Salt water glistening the red decks before running away into the scuppers and draining over the side whence it came. Somewhere from nowhere a bird dipping and swooping on erratic thermals and currents. The stuff of watercolourists. The stuff of seasickness.

What does it? What makes a lad strut the decks, sway with the easy motion from the bridge's wing with clean wind skipping over the varnished dodgers into his innocent, ruddy, spotless face suddenly feel dizzy, full of wretched belch, sucking, horrid swallow, cold sweating and then, in too slowly understood desperation, lunge for a bucket, any bucket. What makes the brightest being, full of life and breeze and adventure and contempt for those who catch buses and trains, slump as some grey dirty bundle, victim to the cruellest, the most undignified malaise? The answer, or so it is said, is a disruption in the middle ear canal which is supposed to control balance. It seems impossible that something as ordinary as a semicircular bit of gristle might be the unpicking of so much carefully fashioned image. Pork dripping sandwiches the night before and a fully fried breakfast on the morning bring spectacular crescendo to the event once begun. So why do some and others do not? Who knows?

Dark-haired Europeans are less likely to get seasick than blonds and blondes. Lean men less likely than tubby ones. Yet skinny Nelson was always ill – even when he had two arms and two eyes. Helmsmen survive longer than winchmen. One's concentrating more on the task.

Maybe it's all a law of averages. An averagely built, averagely fit, averagely active, averagely determined person has most things happen to him – on average. That's most people. They get colds, backaches, miss buses, C-grades in maths, live to their late sixties instead of late thirties or eighties, never get fat, never get thin, have regular inside leg measurements. So if most suffer seasickness at some time, then it's just the average. When they do, they look at those who don't. They seek some sign of what it is that makes these superhumans immune. Immune from being so close to no longer caring if they should survive or not. The danger of losing all sense of care is a terrible symptom. Hanging over the gunwales careless of the mocking power of the sea is rare recklessness in one who, an hour earlier, double-lashed a lantern to the storm halyard, spun tight the dogs on the metal scuttle and deadlights over portholes and rigged lifelines for the cook, who struggled along sloping decks with hot stews. Cures? Sleep and time for the lucky. A quiet life in a country sub-post office for the less fortunate. There are pills and patches. A dose of dry ginger helps. There was a coasting skipper who never went afloat without tins of rice pudding. Swore by the stuff. Cursed when he'd run out. *Mal de mer* sounds better. Whatever the name, there are not many who haven't heard hell chuckle above the sodden sound of the last wisp of bile. A leveller in every sense. Be warned. The smartest-cut jib can crumple in a long Atlantic swell.

### 9 February 1958, a day out of Gib

I knew it was going to happen. I didn't know it was going to happen like that. I wasn't feeling too bad. Then we hit Biscay. I swear the ship was trying to throw me off. We had to rig lifelines along the decks and gangways while we were still in the Channel.

Then bang. Biscay. It was like someone turning the big dipper up full speed and jerk. I was OK on deck. But the Mate saw me and gave me a bollocking and told me to go inside. I managed to get to the bathroom – times like this you forget they're supposed to be heads – and threw up like some old drunk into the Shanks. I thought I felt OK then. I got my oilskin on and held on like a silly bugger until I got to the bridge deck. The Mate was up there. Wanted to know what I thought I was doing. Said I was on watch. Don't be a bloody fool. Get below. I tried to explain that I was better off up here on the wing of the bridge. Go below, he said. You're no friggin' good to me here, Chuck, he says. He calls everyone but the Captain Chuck. I was staggering past the Third Mate's cabin and I just blacked out. It wasn't for long, and I could feel them lifting me on to the smoke room couch. I was half there and half not and felt I had to say something. Like a bloody fool I said the obvious. Where am I? With that, they dropped me where I was. Thought I was bullshitting. Next thing the Captain's passing. Wants to know what the fuck's going on. What am I doing there in my oilskins? Get to your cabin, he said. Off I go again. I crawled the last ten feet. Ainslie's sitting on his bunk smoking a cigar and eating a manky Mars bar. I took one whiff and threw up in the gash can. Ainslie said I was a dirty little bugger and that the Mate said I should be tied between the winches with a bucket of stew on one side and an empty bucket on the other. As I emptied one I would fill the other. This time I missed the bin. Ainslie made me clear it up and said I was the dirtiest little turd he'd ever met. That was three days ago. I'm now feeling great, but Ainslie says he can still smell me everywhere. I've dhobi'd all my gear, but I know what he means. Ainslie, of course, has never been sick in his life. He said, I thought you were a tough old bargehand. I said that we never got as far as Biscay. He said, Pity you got as far as this ship. I'm feeling pretty miserable. At least it's getting warm.

And for a lad barely seventeen, with more spots than whiskers, there was another hazard of rolling decks.

## 9 FEBRUARY 1958

Ainslie says he reckons this trip will be at least eighteen months. I said I thought we were only going to Korea. Ainslie said you don't 'only' go anywhere with this lot. They'll keep you out for so long that you'll forget buses are red. I said, They're green where I came from. Another thing, he said, don't be a smartarse. I thought I'd just be gone for three months. It's a bit difficult. I've only got two razor blades. Ainslie says I don't need those because I don't really shave, do I? He's right, so I'm now shaving every day and making sure that he sees me with the soap on my face. The dangerous bit is when she rolls. I've learned to shave with one hand on the basin. I watched Dad shave, and he pulls down his cheek to make it easier. You can't do that hanging on by your fingernails to the taps in case she ships a green one and you slit your throat in the excitement. So I have to pull faces so that the razor runs smoothly. We had a really ugly kid in our class called Pull-a-Face Benson. I'm getting as good as him. This morning I cut myself three times. The biggest problem is that I've got a couple of spots. Quite a few, really. It must be the food. The Mate says my face looks as mucky as the bum on a pox doctor's clerk. I wanted to ask him how he knew. Didn't, though. I wonder if I should buy one of those electric razors when we get to Gibraltar?

\* \* \*

As each day she'd headed south, the sun had seemed closer until at last the cloud had drifted away. One evening it was there, the next morning it had gone – for the time being. In the minutes between darkness and dawn there were enough stars for the Mate to take a sight and fix the ship's position. This, remember, was an old tramp with none of the so-called modern aids to navigation. Apart from the gyrocompass and an often inaccurate radio beam, navigation was very basic and very good. Keep it simple, Chuck, the Mate would say. There wasn't much option. Yet these seamen had the great advantage over their sailing ancestors – engines. A 7,000-ton ship like The Tramp would be hampered by extremely rough weather. But generally she could maintain a course and a speed that would allow the navigator to estimate the ship's position at any time. There were three ways of getting a more accurate fix of where she was. In sight of land you could take a bearing of heads and nesses and even church spires. With skies clear and the horizon sharp, then every noon the Master and Mates would fix the ship's latitude by taking a sight of the sun. Then in the twilights, when the horizon was sharp and the brightest stars visible, the Mate would measure the altitudes of three or four stars with his sextant, and as long as he knew the time to the second from the ship's chronometer then the position of the ship could be fixed as accurately as his almanacs and tables could calculate, and his pencil could mark the cross.

Now, in early February, The Tramp was far enough south for clear skies, and just off Cape St Vincent she altered to an easterly course and tucked into the Mediterranean and the lad's first foreign port of call, Gibraltar.

He hadn't quite known what to expect. He knew it was 'one of ours', British. In the harbour were a Royal Navy frigate and a couple of minesweepers, a rear admiral's red and white flag fluttering over HMS *Rooke*, the shore base. (It was admiral Sir George Rooke who captured Gibraltar in 1704 with another admiral, Sir Cloudesley Shovel. Somehow, the Royal Navy could not bring itself to calling its Gibraltar headquarters HMS *Cloudesley Shovel*.) English soldiers fit and slim and some filling out their time as conscripts – the end of another military generation. In front of Government House, small cannon and the ceremonial mounted guard, their marching and counter-marching repeated throughout the Crown and constitutional colonies of what was still a large empire. The Rock Hotel, fading in step with the Empire, built for another moment of history and to all appearances waiting to be transported brick by brick to the seafront at Eastbourne. The narrow streets were Spanish but the people fiercely English. Not even Scottish, Welsh or Irish. Being English was less confusing than some explanation of Celtic allegiance. Spanish workers crossed the border at La Linea. The crosspatch of Anglo-Spanish diplomacy was yet to erupt with the sound of clanking chains as the border was closed a decade later.

## 10 FEBRUARY 1958

Arrived in Gibraltar this morning. The rock is there right enough. I've seen lots of pictures and somehow I thought it was going to be bigger. I said so to the Mate and he said, Just how big d'you want the friggin' thing? I told him about the picture I had at home, and he said that when you see everything in books they don't show you what's next to it, so it's never going to look so great. He said the whole world's like that. He said Gib's a nice enough place for a run ashore, but not for long – just a couple of days. I thought it was going to be Spanish. It's not. It's quite warm but it's almost not foreign. The harbour looks foreign and so do some of the people. The Fourth says a lot of Spanish come over the border to get work because they're starving in Spain. They don't look very thin. I said how did he know they were starving, and he said that his brother was in the Spanish Civil War. I asked him when that was. Just twenty years ago, he said. I said, Maybe they've got some food now? He said he doubted it, and when we went ashore I should keep my hand on my money because they were mostly crooks. There are a lot of British soldiers here and quite a few sailors. I saw a warship in the harbour. The Mate said it's one of ours because this is one of the most important places in the world. It guards the entrance to the Atlantic. I asked him who it was guarding against. The Communists, he said. I told him that my Uncle Eric, who according to my mother knows a thing or two about the Communists, says they're already in the Atlantic. That's as maybe, said the Mate, but we're not letting any more in. I can't see what one warship is expected to do, even if it is British.

Ainslie and I couldn't go ashore together because we're only here until the morning. We should have left this afternoon, but we've had to wait overnight because something for the engine room that should have arrived from England hasn't turned up. I don't mind; it let me get ashore. I didn't go far, but in some ways the town's a bit like Folkestone. You can get Marmite here and I expect there's a Woolworth's, although I didn't see one. The policemen are just like ours and they've got proper helmets, like Georgina Ryder's dad in Belvedere, although he has a quite good push-bike and they don't. I saw the Third Engineer ashore. He was buying something for his wife. I said that it was ages before we went home. That's all right, he said, I'll post it. All the way to

Montrose? He said if you did, then you weren't that far. I'm not sure what he meant, but it sounds a good idea. I had to buy an electric razor so I hadn't much money left. Anyway, I found a tie that I think my dad would quite like. It's green with yellow stripes, although I can't remember him wearing a tie except his uniform ones. I bought Mum a green scarf. The Third showed me where the post office was. It's bigger than the one in Bexleyheath Broadway. I suppose it has to be. Probably the only one in the whole country.

He was now broke. The shipping companies, even the old tramping firms, were very paternalistic towards the deck apprentices. He would get in his first year a total of £90 in wages plus a shilling a month washing allowance. But he would be expected to send some of that £90 a year home either to a post office account or perhaps to his parents. As late as the 1950s a son leaving school was expected to bring in a bit of income for the family budget. The fact that the son had gone to sea neither absolved him from that responsibility nor set aside his parents' expectation. So at the beginning of the voyage he had to sign an allotment form that would send £45 of his £90 home to his parents. Therefore, with him just a fortnight into his four years' indentures, the apprentice boy had no moneys to draw and only loose change from what was left of the precious £5 note his father had given him at Liverpool Street Station. He had to get an advance on his wages to buy the electric razor. He'd not be allowed another advance for the whole voyage. He'd spend the rest of the trip trying to figure out how much money he'd have for a run ashore when they reached port. There was a year and a half to go, although he didn't know that. He became quite good at mental arithmetic.

For The Tramp, Gibraltar was not a place to loiter. She was there for bunkers, to take on enough fuel oil and water to get her across the Mediterranean to top up at the Suez Canal, then down the Red Sea and into Aden.

Into the Med did not signal the order to break out the tropical kit. That sea can be horrid. So it was that winter. The sun that had gleamed over her white superstructure off Cape St Vincent was resting. February clouds loitered over the whole western end of the middle sea. In the back of his mind the apprentice boy had an idea that the Mediterranean was always hot. The south of France, Italy, all that desert. And remember we are still in the 1950s. These were the days before mass package holidays, the days before a returning sunbather could be asked, Where did you go? reply, Majorca, be asked, Where's that? and reply, I don't know; I flew there. So to the lad, now coated in his long black shiny oilskin on the wing of the bridge, his impressions of the Mediterranean were glossy pictures and not even hearsay. The passage across the tideless sea was nearly as rough as it had been when the ship crossed that great coastal ledge that drops away into the Atlantic where the two forces of deep and shallow meet on the rim of Biscay.

A day and a bit on, the skies remained grey in the light and impenetrable in the dark – no sun-sights at noon, no star-fixes at twilight. South of Sardinia, leaving Galite Island well to starboard. Then the Sicilian Channel and his first triumph. With no star-sights and only the dead reckoning of the navigators for their position, it was the apprentice boy who in the early-morning half-light picked up the loom and then the beam of the lighthouse on Isola di Pantelleria. The quiet, but not begrudged, 'Well done, Chuck' from the Mate made him feel ten feet tall and for the first time to be truly the son of his seafaring ancestors and a proper part of the crew. But this didn't mean he should get above himself. He'd quickly learned that. And even during the first few weeks, he learned that he was at the bottom of the heap, of which fact the next one up, Ainslie, would never think anything but his solemn duty to remind him. He was no different from the apprentice in the factory. The only thing missing was the blue boiler suit, the flask and the factory hooter at five. The hardest part was what he called the Great Contradiction. He wasn't sure what it meant, but he'd read it somewhere in a book and he had a proper regard for books.

## 13 FEBRUARY 1958

They reckon me and Ainslie are the lowest of the low. Nothing personal, they say, just a fact. Cheap labour on deck. Chipping, scraping, red-leading. So we're not officers but we're not allowed to mix with the Chinese crew, who wouldn't want to mix with us anyway. It's the Great Contradiction. Ainslie says that when we're on the bridge for watches or going in and out of port, we have to get smartened up. Uniform. Soon as we're at sea, it's into working gear. We're cheap deckboys, which is all we are. But then we're not Chinkies, are we? They think we're useless because we don't know as much as they do. The officers think we're useless because we don't know as much as them. The crazy thing is that in four years I could be Third Mate. In fifteen years I could be Master. Maybe not of this ship, but of something. But fifteen years is fifteen years. Today's today and I'm the lowest of the low. Lower than Ainslie, of course. How do I know? Because he said so. Course he did. He said I'm ignorant. And if Ainslie said I am, then it must be true. How do I know that? Because Ainslie says so.

The hardest part of the Great Contradiction is that although everyone says I don't know anything (which is sort of true) they still expect me to do things they say I don't know how to do (and well). When I don't do them well, they give me a bollocking. Ainslie says life's a bugger and the trick is to know who the bugger is. I think what he means is that it's much better to avoid everything and everybody.

I now accept that I'm the lowest of the rotten low. I just wish they wouldn't make it so obvious.

# 5

## EAST OF SUEZ

The weather cheered up. So did he. Now The Tramp was gradually sidling up to the sun. She was running further south and east, leaving Malta to port well north of Khalif Surt and Benghazi, where his Uncle Jack had died with distinction 'in the war'. South of Crete, north of Tobruk, north of Marsa Matruh, where his Uncle Ned had not died from his wounds but often thought it would have been better had he done so. And then, early one morning, Bûr Sa'îd – Port Said, truly the gateway to the Suez Canal, the Red Sea and the Indian Ocean.

### 20 FEBRUARY 1958, PORT SAID

Arrived early this morning, Mate told us to keep our noses clean. I asked why. Ainslie said it was just as he had thought all along: I'm an ignorant little bugger. Didn't I know there had been a war? I told him, Yes, my Uncle Ned was nearly killed in it – he was a

Desert Rat. He called me a pillock. Not that war, he said: Suez. I'd heard of it. But not much. I suppose I must have been playing cricket or something. We were quite busy at school then. I asked the Fourth. He's a policeman, so he should know. He said a couple of years ago the English and the Frogs had tried to capture the Suez Canal from the Gypos, who, he says, are all thieving blighters. Why didn't we then, I asked him. He said, Because we got screwed by the Americans, who refused to be on our side. Never trust the Americans, he said. What about the Egyptians? Don't trust them buggers, he said, and watch your money. As we came into Port Said there's a big statue on the starboard side, or rather there was. The Fourth said that it was some bloke called Lessops [de Lesseps] who built the Canal. That bloke Lessops is lying on his side. The Gypos have pulled him down. The Fourth said they'll leave him there – it's symbolism. I'm not sure what 'symbolism' is, and as Ainslie was there I didn't ask. I said, Lessops doesn't sound like an English name. Ainslie said that's because he was French. I suppose you think we built everything, even the sodding pyramids, he said. I suppose he's right. At school they were always saying how great we were and that was why we were called Great Britain. Pity old Edgington [his history master] couldn't come here.

Such was the Canal's symbolism that it brought about the downfall of more than the statue of Ferdinand, Vicomte de Lesseps. The Canal was opened in 1869 (the year the *Cutty Sark* was built), and in 1875 Disraeli (or at least his henchmen) did some very good business in Cairo with a scoundrel who was the Ottoman representative. Disraeli smiled his thanks and with the contract still damp went to see Queen Victoria. Here you are, Your Majesty, he said (or something similar),

I've bought us a controlling interest in the most important waterway in the world. And it was very, very important, it had cut so much time off the Far East trade passage for steamships.

The big square-riggers, because of their handling difficulties and also the transit charges, still took the longer route in the main. The British had been in Egypt long before the Canal opened and until recently had administered Egypt and the Sudan. The fat king Farouk was kicked out in July 1952 just five and a bit years before the lad arrived in Port Said. The coup was led by General Neguib. But he wasn't long in office. Everyone knew that the colonial change was inevitable. The new regime in Egypt made it clear it was going to take over everything that was British, including what was called the Suez Canal Zone. While the lad was watching Queen Elizabeth's coronation (the first time he'd seen a television), British families were getting out of Egypt as quickly as possible. This was 1953, the year in which the Korean War ended, Edmund Hillary and Sherpa Tenzing reached the top of Mount Everest, Randolph Turpin won the middleweight championship of the world, Len Hutton's England cricketers won the Ashes from Australia and the Goons started. By 1954 the most powerful leader the Middle East had seen, Colonel Gamal Abdul Nasser, was in power in Cairo. Nasser's triumph was nationalism. He forced the British into an agreement to pull out their 60,000 or so troops from their Suez encampments. In 1956, when the lad had first sighted The Tramp from the decks of his sailing barge, the British and the French, helped by the Israelis, sent their soldiers, airmen and sailors back to Suez in an attempt to regain control of the waterway. They failed. Nasser did not. The Americans didn't want to help. It was, or so they thought in Washington, a crazy lunge of colonialism attempting to recapture what it thought was lost greatness. Anthony Eden, the British Prime Minister, fell as fatally as de Lesseps' image. Like the mocked masonry at Port Said, Eden was abandoned by his political friends. Left where he had fallen. The so-called Suez War was, as the Americans had known, the last cavalry charge of British imperialism. The Americans were yet to make theirs.

The lad wouldn't have known anything of this. Not even the Fourth Engineer had grasped the truth of what had happened. There was, in 1958, still the illusion of empire, of owning most of the world, of British Is Best and the Wogs Start at Calais. Suez, war or no war, was foreign to everything the lad had known at first hand or had been taught. At the same time he felt English and therefore superior. His inbred sense of superiority had been nurtured at home, at school, on the wireless, in magazines, in overheard conversations. With such unwitting arrogance came great expectation. No wonder, then, that to the lad Port Said and Suez were the first places on the voyage that were truly in the picture books. Dust, camels, a quieter dignity and, for the first time, that sense that northern Europeans were rarely prepared for in the 1950s, of a society not formed about the Christian Church. Yes, truly different.

## 20 FEBRUARY 1958, SUEZ

You can't see much from the ship except all the buildings are cream and white. There are loads of people along the wall who seem to be just sitting there or standing around doing nothing. A lot of them wear long nightshirt things and some are wearing sort of red flowerpots on their heads, just like in the pictures. The Fourth called them fezzes. It's strange actually seeing them. They don't fit right down like Dad's cap or trilby, but none of them seems to fall off. It's all very slow, not like our docks where everything happens, or in Amsterdam (or was it Rotterdam? I

still don't really know – I shall have to look back in the logbook).
I was standing by the gangway waiting for the agent to come
aboard with the chief steward. He's Chinese and I asked him
what he thought of the Egyptians. He started shaking his head.
Crazy people. Crazy people. He didn't say why and when I told
Ainslie he said that the Chinese always say that about everyone
and then do business with them. He said that he would bet that
there's a big Chinatown in Cairo or somewhere. But that's not
what I was interested in. I know what I think of foreigners because
I don't know many. I think they're different because they are and
because we've more or less been in charge of them for hundreds
of years. A lot of them belong to us and the Queen. So it's easy to
be British and know what you think of foreigners. But what no
one has ever told me is what foreigners think of each other.

The business of Canal transit was complicated and slow. It was an act
of waiting, entertainment and then a slow-motion cavalcade when
the great ships proceeded in line ahead with the sedate near silence of
the camel train seen off Ismailia.

## 20 FEBRUARY 1958, SUEZ CANAL

There are ships everywhere all waiting to go into the Canal but
it's not very wide and so we have to wait for the other lot coming
north before we can go south.

We're tied up midstream at buoys. We'd hardly got the moorings out before the bumboats were alongside. The Mate said to
make sure all the cabins were locked and the ports shut. He said
the bumboatmen were a thieving lot of bastards. The Fourth
said that's because they're foreign anyway. I bet he was a good

policeman. About half a dozen of the bumboatmen were allowed on board. There was this bloke in a long nightshirt and a brown sports jacket. He said he was gully-gully man. He's quite old, older than Dad and he hasn't shaved for three or four days by the looks of him, and he's got this sort of white speckly whiskers and strange brown teeth which are all crooked. He said, would I like a cigarette and I told him I don't smoke. Big laugh. He thought that was very funny. He said all sailors smoke. He's a sort of conjuror and he's got a load of chicks and he makes them disappear and then come back again out of his sleeve and even his top pocket. Then he put his hand behind my ear and next thing this little yellow thing is going tweet-tweet or something. Ainslie said keep your hands in your pockets otherwise he'll have your balls coming out of his turban. The gully-gully man just laughed and said to me, You give me money. I said I hadn't got any. He then said did I want dirty pictures and I said I hadn't got any money. Another one of them came up with a basket. He's got some really nice wallets with old Egyptian pictures on them. Square sort of people walking sideways with one arm in front like a snake and the other behind like a crooked tail. The Fourth said the pictures are 4,000 years old. He bought a big leather pouf with the same sort of pictures. Wouldn't mind a wallet, but Ainslie says they're rubbish and, anyway, he said, what did I want a wallet for if I hadn't got any money? He said he hoped I wasn't going to turn out to be a mean bastard. Another one was waiting by number four hatch when we came back for smoke-o. He kept looking over his shoulder and seemed only to be able to speak out of the corner of his mouth. You want Spanish Fly, he said. Ainslie told him to poke off. But I have bought a camera. Its called an Agfa Isolette. It looks new and it's got bellows. Ainslie said it probably doesn't work. I don't know, I forgot to buy any film. Too late now. We're going through the Canal tonight. Ainslie wanted to know where I got the money. I said I swapped it for that blue jacket I bought in wherever it was, Amsterdam or Rotterdam. He said I was a pillock, what did I expect to go ashore in? I said it was hot enough not to wear a jacket. He said I'm still a pillock – but he reckoned it was OK as the thing still stinks from when I was sick down it. I thought it best to change the subject and I told him I asked the gully-gully man about this Suez war thing. He said if the Mate heard me say that he'd take a knife to my wotsits and show me a couple of tricks with them that the gully-gully man never thought possible. Ainslie's pretty crude, but I laughed. He likes that.

There were two convoys. One sailed north from Port Suez and this one south from Port Said. The Canal was narrow, sometimes less than 200 feet across, until it widened towards its southern end into the Bitter Lakes.

Late at night the southbound convoy made ready to leave Port Said. A huge lantern rigged on the bow. On the bridge, the Master, the Third Mate, the deck apprentice, the senior quartermaster on the wheel and a bluff, heavy-booted man in a white plastic cap. This was the pilot, the one who knew every depth of the Canal, every signal. The one to advise the Master. In practice the one to tell him what to do. Gone were the days of the expatriate French and British pilots. Times and Nasser, British and French illusions, had changed all that. The pilot who leaned against the varnished wheelhouse corner window, constantly chewing blackcurrant pastilles and clearing his thick clogged throat, was a Russian. The Soviet Union, new colonists. It would take a little time, but they, too, would be thrown out.

The excitement of travelling through the Canal for the first time would keep the lad awake as the silent procession moved south, passing seemingly deserted villages and, on the starboard side, Ismailia, the southern extent of the British army's Suez adventure. On the port side, the Sinai Desert. That, too, was Egyptian. For the moment. This was 1958. In less than a decade it would be stormed by the tanks of an Israeli general, Moshe Dayan, and taken for the Israeli state, which even by then would be but less than 20 years old.

## 21 FEBRUARY 1958, SUEZ CANAL

The pilot is a Communist and he's a very big one. Sort of an upright oval shape. He's got a uniform cap which I think is made of plastic. It's like a huge, cream dinner-plate. He doesn't say very much, and I don't think he speaks much English. What happens if we get into trouble I'm not sure. He doesn't smile much and keeps asking for mugs of tea and condensed milk. Just before he gives an order, he makes a funny noise in his throat. Pop [his grandfather] used to make the same noise before he spat in the fire. The pilot spits into the Canal. I think the Captain doesn't trust him much and has stayed on the bridge all the time, just walking up and down and then crossing from side to side. When we let go the buoys in Port Said, the Captain said he wanted steam on deck. That means there's steam to the for'd windlass all the time in case we had to let go the anchor. There must be fifty or so ships in this convoy. If one stopped, the others would have a bit of a job standing off. It's a pretty straightforward bit of pilotage, I would have thought. You don't need to know much once you're in the Canal. Just keep going. Follow the ship in front and keep a safe distance on Slow Ahead. It's not as if there was a buoyed channel or hidden banks. If there are, there's not much we could do about it, and the ship in front of us is much bigger and probably has a deeper draught, so we should be OK. But the Mate says you have to have a pilot because those are the rules. He says that the Communists are good sailors and that before they killed the tsar they were our friends and that our king and their tsar were cousins. And he said the pilot's on to a good thing. He said the Reds are now running Egypt since we got kicked out and that the pilot probably has a better life than at home. According to him, they're all peasants and not very bright. So I asked him, if they're all dim, how come they managed to launch the Sputnik last year and the Yanks couldn't, and how come they're running the Gypos and we're not? He said it's all part of what he calls the Communist Threat. The pilot doesn't look much of a threat to me. I think he looks like Dad's brother, Uncle George – except for the plastic hat, of course.

Sixteen or so hours on, now in daylight, The Tramp was in the Bitter Lakes. The lanterns were sent ashore, the northbound convoy came through, and soon the engine room telegraph clanged Slow Ahead into the final cut and then, with a burst of freedom, Full Ahead into the Gulf of Suez and then the Red Sea.

The warm sun over Arabia meant the ship could relax into its normal sea routine before reaching Port Sudan, and so the apprentice, except for mealtimes, put away his soft cotton and climbed into the still-stiff dungarees and work shirt.

## 22 FEBRUARY 1958, RED SEA

I like being on the bridge better than on deck. It's not the uniform, and I don't much mind getting dirty and that, it just seems that we're cheap labour. Most of the stuff like chipping and scraping the sailors could do. That's what they sign on for. Also, I'm not very good at it. Ainslie says I haven't a clue and I'm too slow. The Mate says he'll put me on job and finish if I don't smarten my ideas up. He said something which *may* be true. He said the whole point about being on deck is that you get to know everything about the ship. He said that if you have to grease blocks and wires, chip foredecks, paint hatch coamings and all the rest of it, then you begin to understand two things: you find out what needs to be done just to keep the ship safe and going, and you know what it takes and how long it takes to do it all.

So, according to the way he explained it, when one day I'm the Mate I'll have done it all, so I'll know what needs doing and I'll know how to get the best out of the crew who have to do it. I told Ainslie what he'd said. He said he reckoned I wouldn't be a Mate as long as I had a hole in my bum. I didn't take any notice. It's his way. Always attacking. I said I thought it was pretty good of the Mate to explain something like that.

Ainslie said the Mate was all right, but he wouldn't tell me again. He would give you the benefit of the doubt, once. Then he'd give you the benefit of his fist. I don't believe that, but I know what he means. I think the Mate's quite kind. Not at all what I expected him to be like. He's got a big beard and belly and can look quite tough. And most of all he's the Mate and I'm just a deck apprentice. So he's probably right and I'm probably wrong even if I'm right. It's like the lime juice.

Last night, I had a look at the lime juice. It's in half-gallon bottles and the one I opened had BOARD OF TRADE 1944 on it. But I suppose lime juice doesn't go off. That's the whole point of it. I mentioned the date to the Mate, who said the stuff's strong enough to clean the brass. But he says I should drink it. It's good for scurvy. I said I haven't got scurvy. Must work then, he said. But I've never had scurvy, I said. Just keep drinking the frigging stuff, he said, and you'll never know the half of it.

## 25 FEBRUARY 1958, PORT SUDAN

The Fourth says this is another place that used to belong to us. We'd been in charge with the Egyptians. I said, I thought the Gypos don't like us? He said, That's right; the whole thing's a cockup. We should never have got involved. Anyway, he said that a couple of years ago Sudan became independent. I said I knew all about Gordon of Khartoum in 18-something or other. He said it was Gladstone's fault. That sounds about right. Dad always blames the government for everything, and I suppose the Victorians were no different.

We've come all the way here from Amsterdam light ship just to load salt. We're taking it to Korea. Can't think what they need it for. The salt goes straight in. It's like loading coal. The problem is that everything sweats below and I suppose the salt can rot the ship's sides. For the past few days we've been painting the holds down below with some silver stuff. When we came alongside, we had to pick up extra cargo boards. They're about ten feet long and nine inches deep. They slot into brackets down in the hold and gradually we build up a sort of wooden inner wall. Seems we've got to wait a couple of days before we start loading. Heard the Captain telling the Mate that 'as per bloody usual, Mister, the bloody nig-nogs aren't bloody ready'.

The port routine was different from being at sea. There was no need to keep watches, so most of the ship went on to what it called day-watches, office hours. The only change to this might come if a cargo was being discharged or loaded twenty-four hours of the day, and then the Mates and apprentices went on to a rota to keep cargo-watch. It was the ship's responsibility to make sure that the cargo was stowed properly, and that the cargo-watch was around should there be an accident and to make sure the dockers weren't stealing anything. The assumption of the crew was that wharfies, as they called them, were thieving bastards. Doors locked, scuttles screwed down. The more foreign a wharfie – that is, the blacker – then the more likely he was to be a thief. The lad was told that in his first week. The world was full of foreigners. He suffered also the confusion that although as an Englishman in the late 1950s he was naturally superior to foreigners, he also believed that black men possessed mystical powers. In short, he was frightened of them. Why not? Had he not been told as a tiny child that if he didn't behave himself then the bogeyman would come and get him? The bogeyman was black. When he returned to his locked cabin he would still check everything. The black wharfie could voodoo things away.

## 27 FEBRUARY 1958, PORT SUDAN

Went ashore to the church this morning. It's not for the local people, who are all black, and I suppose they have their own place to go. It's the Mission to Seamen chapel and doesn't have any windows. Very cool, and you look straight out at the desert. There was a camel outside and he kept making quite strong noises. Bit like a donkey. I tried to work out if he was doing it every time the vicar said anything important. He didn't. Which was a pity because I'd have liked to tell Ainslie that it had. Probably wouldn't have believed me anyway.

After Communion the parson took us next door to his sort of vicarage and we had scrambled eggs. He didn't make them. He has a steward, a black servant, and the parson, who I suppose is really a chaplain although I'm not sure what the difference is, said that it had taken two years to train the steward to make scrambled eggs like that. They're quite white and very fluffy. I've never had scrambled eggs before. Fried is what we usually have at home, and boiled at Easter with faces painted on them. The vicar says he likes a drop of whisky in them. His name is Mr Martin, or it might be Martin something or other. I'm not sure. I was the only one there from our ship, but there were some in uniforms from other ships, including a Captain, who seemed really nice. When I told him it was my first trip he wished me luck. Odd. He's the only one who has ever done that. People at home didn't say much. Pop wanted to know when I'd be back. Mum said I should write if I got a moment. I can't remember what Dad said, but I think he'd have said more if he'd known what to say. The Reverend Maxwell said I should say my prayers and that he'd say some for me. I suppose that's the same as wishing me luck. I think I feel a bit homesick.

The Mission to Seamen was known as the Flying Angel because of its emblem. It was very Church of England when it started in the 1850s to look to the spiritual needs of vulnerable Protestant matelots. The Roman Catholics went to the Stella Maris centres for confession and cakes. For some reason, the Catholics always had cakes, whereas the Protestants had bottles of beer and paste sandwiches. There was a Flying Angel meeting room, a chapel and often an ordained chaplain in every major port in the world. The Church ministering to the needs of what was for more than a century the greatest maritime nation ever known. The ship would dock and on board would come the chaplain or whoever. Mostly they were good types, understanding, not evangelists. They'd organise picnics and ping-pong. Nothing churchy, but it was a way of keeping the hard-up and indifferent out of trouble. Some of the chaplains were enthusiasts and very popular and known to sailors all over the world. Some of them appeared surplus to requirement of a British colonial system preparing with unseemly haste to abandon its former charges before it was violently ejected. Most of them lived quite well: a few servants, always cold beers to hand, usually very good scrambled eggs.

## 5 MARCH 1958, PORT SUDAN

The Fourth says the locals here are called fuzzy-wuzzies (I think that's right). I asked him to spell it and he said it didn't matter, a fuzzy-wuzzy was a fuzzy-wuzzy however you spelled him. It's because of their hair. It looks like a wig. Really big and loads of tight curls. During smoke-o this morning, they were lying on the hatch boards picking nits out of each other's head. Quite a few boys at school had nits, but we never picked them. They're all very tall and quite thin and very black. (The blokes, not the nits. I wonder if that's where nitwit comes from?) The Fourth said that that's what Sudan means in the local lingo. Land of the Blacks. I said I thought they looked like royalty. The Fourth said I was just to remember that these were the blighters who killed General Gordon. Perhaps, but most of them don't look as if they've got the energy to kill nits, never mind a general.

There's not much to see in Port Sudan. I suppose it's a bit like

Tilbury and Woolwich. The docks never look like the country. I had a look on the map and the capital, Khartoum, must be 1,000 miles away. Pity. I'd like to have gone there, although the Fourth says the British are not popular.

I've only been to four places so far, Holland, Gibraltar, Egypt and Sudan, and it seems that two of them don't like us. That's half. We're going to Korea next and we've just been at war with them. If the rest of the world's like that, then all that stuff at school and everything Mr Churchill said about us being the best in the world is rubbish. Certainly half the world thinks so and we've done our best to prove they're right.

Just as his elders were wondering who had 'won' the Second World War after all, so the lad was sensing that 'Rule, Britannia!' was slightly out of tune. Surely not. Surely. From Port Sudan The Tramp now headed south to Aden – another verse in the musty Britannic hymnal. As they let go fore and aft from Sudan, they faced about three days' pleasant steaming, keeping well to the east of the Dahlak Archipelago, through the Bab el Mandeb and then round the corner to Aden for bunkers. Three days for the lad to shine and then, well, not to shine.

## 6 MARCH 1958, RED SEA

Good to be back at sea. I've been learning Morse signalling on the Aldis lamp. I learned to do flag semaphore and the Morse Code in the Sea Cadets in Bexleyheath, but I didn't tell anyone on board. So when I was given all the dots and dashes to learn I didn't even bother to look at them. The next day I was up on the bridge on the four to eight watch with the Mate and he wanted to know how I was getting on. I said, Not bad. You'll have to be friggin' better than not bad, Chuck, he said, and started to test me. I walked it. Friggin' hell, he says. Dit-dit-dah-dit, dit-dah-dit, dit-dit, dah-dah-dit, dah-dah-dit, dit-dit, dah-dit. Dit-dit-dit-dit, dit, dit-dah-dit-dit, dit-dah-dit-dit. Friggin' hell.

A minor triumph. Would have been best to leave it at that. He was not that bright.

## 7 MARCH 1958, RED SEA

Made a bit of a cock of the Morse. Early this morning it was still dark and I was on watch with the Mate. There was a ship going the other way three points on the starboard bow. She called us up on the lamp. What ship? Where bound? The Mate said, Go on, Chuck, try your hand. I suppose I was a bit cocky. I got on the lamp and signalled back as fast as I could: ship's name and that we were from Port Sudan bound for Kunsan with salt. I reckoned my Morse was good and pretty fast. What I didn't know was that the other boat was a warship. They've got yeomen who do nothing else but signal. She answered just as fast as I'd sent. Couldn't read a flipping word of it. That'll teach you, Chuck, said the Mate. He took the lamp and signalled back. He could read it right enough. Lesson one, he said: always signal at the speed you want them to send back to you. Lesson two: don't friggin' show off. Lesson three: that's what life's about.

Aden. Still British, on a bright, hot, sunny morning. Sort of. Even the Fourth Engineer had to admit that. The Turks had had it for about 300 years until Britain annexed it – as the nineteenth-century diplomatic argot had it – in 1802. It was of the utmost importance to

Britain even then. Four years earlier, Nelson had defeated the French at Aboukir Bay. This was the famous Battle of the Nile, which, among other things, effectively ended Napoleon's ambitions for a route to the East. There was no Suez Canal in 1802, and Aden was an extremely valuable staging post for Africa and, by the age of steam, an essential coaling station for the Indian Ocean and beyond. The Crown reshuffled its possessions before the Second World War, and in 1937 Aden became a crown colony and remained so for twenty-five years. It was still that when The Tramp sailed in, and although it became part of Saudi Arabia five years later, in 1963, it all ended in bloodshed in the South Yemen revolution four years on and British troops were finally chased out of Aden in November 1967. But that was nine years away. When The Tramp tied up, the talk was not of revolution but of the Little Aden harbour master's pet cheetah. There was much speculation about which – harbour master or cheetah – would tire first of the other.

### 9 MARCH 1958, ADEN

This place looks like the moon. The Fourth says it is. He says there's a place here called The Crater. The Third Mate says it's just Crater. No 'the' in it. Whatever it's called, the Fourth's brother knows all about it. The Fourth's always got someone who knows all about everything. He's one of those people who think they have to tell you what someone else says. That way you believe them because you never have to guess if you think they're smart enough to know, only if they know someone who is. All the teachers were like that. They were always saying what someone else said. Anyway, the Fourth says that his brother's in the army here. Ainslie says his brother's probably a mercenary. I don't think so. I said, Why do we have the army here? The Fourth says it's because the British run the place. I can't think why anyone would bother. The Fourth says it's all about the Horn of Africa and protecting interests. Our interests are getting bunkers. The harbour water is green and you can smell the bunker oil right across the water. There's row after row of ships tied up. No one goes ashore. It's what the Fourth says it's always been, just a place to refuel. The blokes who do the oil barges are not like the ones in Suez. They're a different lot. Quicker. Sharper. The bumboats have got the same things. Wallets and flip-flops and cameras. I tried to buy a film for the camera I bought in Suez. Didn't have any. Ainslie says it's because the camera won't work. He says they're all in it together. Probably cousins. You buy the camera and they all agree not to sell any film so you can't complain because you don't know. Sometimes Ainslie can be really thick. I said I'd wait until I got to Singapore. Probably got cousins there as well. He reckons there won't be a single place in the whole wide world that I'll be able to get film. We've only been here a couple of hours and we're leaving in twenty minutes. Shame. I think if you've just come for bunkers and haven't got ashore, then you can't count it as a place you've been to.

# 6

## 'NATIVES FRIENDLY, WATER OBTAINABLE'

Crossing the Indian Ocean was the time to settle into a long sea-going routine. At ten knots flat out, The Tramp let you do that. The fast Blue Funnel, Ben boats and Ellermans had hardly cleared one fairway buoy before they were wondering whether it was port or starboard side to at the next port. Later, when sailing the Pacific, he would come to treasure the relaxed routine of working on deck and then night-watches on the bridge. The ship would be clean. The cabin doors for ever open. White shorts and shirts drying in minutes in tropical sunlight. Sleeping on the boat deck. Not quite the Belvedere marshes and the mud foreshore of Long Reach. He could cope with that.

### 11 MARCH 1958, OFF SOCOTRA

Off Socotra this morning. I looked it up in the pilot book.

'Natives friendly, water obtainable' it said. Wonder when that was written?

One of the Blue Funnel Line ships went by this morning. Not sure where she came from. I saw her coming into Aden as we were leaving. She must have been there for a couple of days. She was going like a train. Half again as fast as us. Maybe fifteen knots. We're doing no more than ten. It's about as fast as we can go, although the Mate says he's known 260 miles in a day, but not often and probably only in a stream. He said that some of the Blue Funnel boats do seventeen knots. No wonder they get to the Far East and back to England in three or four months. Ainslie calls Blue Funnel, Blue Flue. Nice-looking ship. Black hull. All the accommodation amidships. Square. Carries twenty passengers. I bet that's better than going on a liner. Auntie Joyce went out to Australia on a liner and the cabins were small cupboards three decks below the waterline. Ainslie says Blue Flue's been around more than a hundred years. Strange name. *Agamemnon*. Ainslie says they're all Greek names. Why's she registered in Liverpool, then, if she's Greek? He says she's not. Started a hundred years ago by someone called Holt. Just liked Greek names. I said how did he know? Turns out Ainslie's cousin's Third Mate in the *Pelus* or something. Would be, wouldn't he? Mind you, he's got a Mate's ticket. Our Third Mate hasn't got any ticket. He was an apprentice last trip. Bet you wouldn't get anyone with a ticket to come Third Mate in this ship. I like it. But it'd be nice to do just three months then home. Blue Flue's the thing, one day, although Ainslie says you have to have been at sea school, somewhere like the Worcester or Pangbourne, before they'll take you. It's like Dad says, to get the best things you've got to go to the posh schools.

Mum says he's a Socialist bleeder, but I think he's right.

There were two watch systems. Day-watches and bridge-watches. Bridge-watches were on a four-hour system, midnight to four, four to eight and eight to noon and so on. At sea, the apprentice would usually be used as a deckhand during the day and then keep one of the bridge-watches at night as dogsbody, tea-maker, runner and lookout to one of the Mates. The junior apprentice, our lad from Kent, would find himself for the first part of this voyage standing watch with the Mate – the chief or first officer. He would go on at four in the morning. The apprentice coming off the watch would shake him at 3.45 and he'd have fifteen minutes to get to the bridge washed, shaved and hopefully still awake. He'd be there until eight and then, after breakfast, turn to in his working gear as a deckhand.

The day-watches meant a normal industrial day. The senior apprentice would have been to see the Mate, who would have handed out the jobs for the day. There was nothing very glamorous. Seamanship is a craft. Chipping and scraping the decks. Slapping on gooey red lead to keep the saltwater rust at bay. Sand and canvassing the boat oars. Best of all for the lad, knotting and splicing ropes, sticking and sewing heavy canvas, greasing, raking and reeving block and tackle. 'Tay-kel', not tackle, said the Mate. Taykel. Got it? Yes, sir. Never 'tackle'. Tackle was for frigging fishermen. Then there was his hammock.

## 12 MARCH 1958, INDIAN OCEAN

Got to make a hammock. It doesn't look that difficult, but Ainslie made a big thing of it. He says as I've spent all this time in a barge, I should be able to do it without looking. He said he's surprised I wear shoes. Wonders why I'm not shinning up the mast before breakfast and hanging on the forestay by my toenails. Wish I never mentioned the barge. He showed me his hammock. He may be a bit grim but he knows what he's doing. It's really neat, although there can't really be much to it. All you do is get eight feet of boat canvas, stitch the ends over in a hem like a girl's frock and then bang brass eyes in. The clever bit is eye-splicing the rope to it. This morning had to see the Chinkie casab for some canvas. He's a miserable bugger. Anyone would think all the stores were his personally. He kept saying something like, What you want this fashion? I said it was for a hammock. He said, Hammock no belong ship pigeon. Belong you pigeon. He doesn't speak much English. Ainslie calls it pigeon English. I said, why pigeons? He said because it is. He always says that when he doesn't know.

## 13 MARCH 1958, INDIAN OCEAN

The hammock took quite a time. The back joint in my thumb is red raw. You have to use a thing called a palm. It's a strip of bull hide which slips over your thumb and then runs across the palm of your hand. There's a round steel bit about the size of a shilling with pockmarks which fits just by the fat bit of the thumb. That's where you push the needle through the canvas. Problem is, every time you push, the hole on top of the thumb rubs like stink. It's actually bleeding. Or was. Ainslie got some iodine and splashed it on and I went screaming mad. Ainslie said I was a big sissy and should be doing dressmaking. And he didn't think much of the stitching, although he couldn't say much about the splicing. Frank Bevan taught me to splice, and he only had three fingers on his right hand and could do it better than anyone Ainslie knows. At least he said it was not bad, which is about as nice as he's ever likely to be.

## 15 MARCH 1958, STILL IN THE INDIAN OCEAN

So Ainslie's got it wrong about this pigeon English. It's not that at all. I asked the Fourth. Surprising what these old blokes know. He says it's pidgin, not pigeon. Why, I said. He said it goes back to the 1600s and something when the English first came across the Chinkies. Fourth says I mustn't call them Chinkies. I said why not and he said because it's disrespectful. I said it wasn't. Leastways, I didn't think so. He said not to be so rude, they're just as good as we are. Well I know that, that's why they're Chinkies. It's nice to call them something that's different. Just like Dad calls the blokes on the buses darkies and niggers. Doesn't mean he doesn't like them. Fourth said if he caught me saying niggers he'd have me up in front of the Captain. Maybe he's right. Anyway, this word pidgin means 'business'. When the CHINESE!!!! tried to say 'business', they couldn't. It came out as 'pidgin'. So that's why we say, it's not my pidgin, only my dad's just like Ainslie and he says it's not my pigeon. Sounds about right.

The Fourth always looks as if he knows what he's talking about. It's quite difficult sometimes. Everyone knows more than me. I suppose they have to. They're older and they've done quite a lot, even Ainslie who really knows a lot and is very, very good at everything we have to do. Being at sea is not about being a sailor. It's about taking orders and assuming that whoever's above you knows more than you do. Dad says that when he was in the army, officers never really knew what was going on. I'm not so sure. If officers tell you what to do, then that's what's going on, so they must know.

Taking orders wasn't a difficult task for the lad. In the 1950s obedience was still a reasonable proposition for most people. Where the lad lived, the doctor, headmaster and parson were still called 'Sir' to their faces. They were the three people in the village who everyone knew had to have education. They were more than middle class. The stethoscope could hear damned well near into your soul, the blackboard was still the prime number of knowledge, and the parson's verses and text preached solemn obeisance. Accent was still important, vocabulary more so. To the lad, authority used words that he never could because he had neither the learning nor the office for them to be credible coming from his lips. His mother could see spots and say 'chickenpox', but only the doctor, saying the same words, made them official. In the classroom he could do his best. Only the teacher could conjugate the verbs to praise or to punish. His mother and father could say their prayers, indeed read them from the Book of Common Prayer. Only the parson had the authority to use the most sacred vocabulary of the Blessing. So the lad understood position and place in whatever society he found himself, particularly because he was an only child. The only child in the 1950s understood blame and guilt.

If there was an untidy bedroom, it could only be his. If something was broken, it could only be his fault. He learned to anticipate guilt and be guilty even when he was innocent. In his life, parents didn't dote. They both worked and truly would have found life easier without a child. Apart from anything else, parents found an only child harder to look after than two or maybe three. It was like having one dog. Two are easier. They amuse each other. He felt guilty because his parents always had to be thinking what to do with him or about him. But if he did something himself, then he felt guilty because he hadn't told them. This was the early 1950s. Parents still had rights to know. The only child could feel left out because he was just that – left out.

If he felt hard done by, told off or generally fed up, there was no brother to hit, talk to, be cruel to or seek sympathy from. So the only child invented worlds of his own but still lived with the downside and showed it and therefore stretched parents, who after all had no training in being mothers and fathers. When an only child went to a friend's house and the friend had siblings, then he either felt an intruder and uncertain or tried to join in with the mood of the moment. But he wasn't of the same lodge and persuasion, so overreacted, showed off, made things up, went away exhilarated and then became so easily downhearted. He couldn't do that at sea. There was no home to go to. In these years, a youngster was not expected to have confidence. Too easily confused with cockiness. He was simply expected to be good at what he was asked to do.

## 17 MARCH 1958

I don't think you have to be brilliant to be on deck. There's no magic in greasing blocks or chipping decks. You simply have to be OK at it. The real threat isn't the Mate, as I thought, but Ainslie, or whoever else is alongside. If we have to chip a bit of deck, then I've got to do it as well as him and as quick as him. If I don't, he has to chip more than me, and because he's senior then he thinks he shouldn't. And if I'm not much good, then he can say so and there's not much I can do about it. I'm not sure I want to spend much more time being told if I'm any good simply by the amount I can chip and scrape a foredeck in a forenoon.

\* \* \*

Always someone more important than you, usually a lot more important. Just like the district officer in the dying colonial service of the 1950s, the apprentice boy's station in life was at best mock Tudor and probably somewhat semidetached. His status was his colour and nationality and what he represented. In the ship's social wiring diagram, he was at the end of a dotted line that eventually led to the officers' accommodation, not to the lower deck. Like that district officer, any authority he had was only local, and even then he had to beware the temper of the local chief – in the apprentice boy's case, the bosun. Among his own people, the apprentice had to watch his place. For example, he was never allowed to eat with the officers in the saloon. Instead, he and Ainslie sat at a corner table in the smoke room and ate their food quickly before the off-duty mates and engineers came in to smoke and chat among themselves.

He knew also that in the name of his nautical education he was on call whenever calling was done. If there were lousy jobs, then the Mate would call for an apprentice. If there was gangway duty when others were ashore, then the Mate would call for an apprentice. Should they attempt to take refuge in the company of the Chinese crew, then they would be upbraided by the Mate. Act like a deckhand, he once said, then you'll be treated like one. Perhaps shore leave stopped. The crew, especially the bosun, the casab in his storeroom, and the chippie regarded them as useless and with a certain amount of amusement because sometimes they were.

Clearly, for the apprentice the most important man on board was not the Captain but the Mate. The Mate kept the ship running above decks. He interpreted the law. He told the crew when to keep watches, what watches to keep, when to chip and scrape and paint, when they could stand down, when they could go ashore. *If* they could go ashore. At sea, he kept the four to eight watches in the morning and evening. So he was up by a quarter to four in the morning at the latest and he probably didn't get to bed until nine, maybe ten at the earliest at night. During the day he might nap in the afternoon, but chances were that he was attending to the day-to-day management of the ship. The Mate was special: works manager to the crew, housemaster to the apprentice boy. Certainly not first-name terms, but always an idea somewhere that he had your interests at heart – wherever that was. Anyone below the Mate didn't really matter, not even the Second Mate. He was just the Second Mate, someone who kept to himself and his gyrocompass and was hardly seen except on the midnight to four and twelve to four watches and maybe on cargo-watch in port.

The deck apprentice's life was not all sand and canvas, chipping, scraping and painting bulkheads, scuppers and winch guards. The Mate expected the company to have sent him a reasonably intelligent youth. To be on the safe side, he regarded him as a fool until he was certain the company had got it right. This wasn't a bad policy. A stupid lad told to paint the poop-deck rails as they steamed at ten knots across the Pacific was just as likely to disappear over the side with hardly a splash as he was to slip behind the starboard ventilator for a quick smoke. Assuming that the clown was no fool, it was from this lad and his like that would come future Mates and Masters. Others might have Milton, Shakespeare and the Bible or even George Bernard Shaw at their bedside, but the lad probably kept *Nicholls's Concise Guide to Navigation*, *Nicholls's Seamanship and Nautical Knowledge for Second Mates, Mates' and Masters' Examination* (always known simply as *Brown's* after one of the authors), *Ship Construction & Stability*, *Jones's Principles for Second Mates*, *Norie's Nautical Tables* and, without question, *Rules & Regulations for the Prevention of Collision at Sea.* These were the handbooks of his life even if his instincts might prove him to be a better examination candidate in the works and life of Mickey Spillane.

His chipping hammer abandoned for a few hours, he would grapple not with rust properties and the application of red lead on stanchions, but definitions and theories unimagined in his Kentish village schoolroom. Right ascension angles rubbed feint-ruled margins with cofferdam construction; compass variation and deviation with lights and shapes for vessels not under command; azimuths with stowage factors; cirrocumulus and cumulonimbus with winter North Atlantic load line; sidereal with Turk's-heads; clove hitch with canopies; lead line leather marks with Sirius, Arcturus and Pollux.

To stow a cargo that wouldn't shift in the next gale between Valparaíso and Cape Town (and there'd be one for sure); to tie a bowline one-handed while dangling over the side on a wobbly painting stage; to strip and repair a damaged davit (or realistically to hold the Third's spanner while he did it); to run out fresh hawsers and shift ship on a wet, miserable Hamburg night: to do all these were the signs of a well-taught seaman. There was a greater prize: the knowledge of navigation.

To leave behind the fairway buoy of a busy and safe port where the pilot went home to his tea, and then to plot and set a course, to check with a day's run, to 'shoot' the noon sun for a latitude, to find four good clear stars and a clean-cut horizon just before the sun rose or not long after it had set and so fix The Tramp's position in the ocean, and to do so day after day after day until one night he could say that at four in the morning to come they'd pick up the loom of the lighthouse of their destination, and for it to come about as he had said, now that was something very special . . .

Dead reckoning. Estimated position. Noon latitude. Day's run. Position. All were everyday happenings, of course. All very ordinary.

To most. Never to the lad. Long, long after those days, he would sail his sloop blind through five dank nights and on the hour of the next morning maybe fetch up three miles and a couple of cables from another fairway buoy. He would still experience the thrill of that first fix of four sharp stars somewhere in the Indian Ocean. Forty years before? Must have been. Just as easy to get lost. The ocean still as big.

## 19 MARCH 1958, INDIAN OCEAN BOUND FOR SINGAPORE

Mate gave us sextant practice today. He says my sextant's old-fashioned. It's called a vernier sextant. Noah used one, says the Mate. So did my Great-Uncle Elliot, I said. This one. The Mate says I should get one of the micrometer sextants. They're modern. Easier to use because the scale's easier to work out – just like a clean ruler, he says. He says everyone has one. I tried to look keen. He gave me one of his looks that he joins up with a big sigh. This Great-Uncle Elliot, he said, bit of a hero was he? I don't know. Shouldn't think so. So I said he was. Felt quite proud at that. Didn't know your family were navigators, Chuck, he says. That got me a bit. They're not. Never have been, except Great-Uncle Elliot, and I'm not really sure about him. I think he ended up as an inshore fisherman, then became a fishmonger, just like Dad's dad. Not much use for a sextant when you're fetching a bit of sole or gutting a hake. Maybe he never did go round the Horn. Maybe he *found* the sextant. Maybe someone had lost it. The Mate says the little arrow on it means that it was War Department property. So was a lot of stuff in Dad's shed. He had a rifle from the war, which he didn't know what to do with and ended up burying at the bottom of the garden. Didn't think I knew. But it wasn't that big a garden. Glad he didn't bury the sextant. I like it wherever it came from.

I like the brass quadrant. I'm getting the hack of it. It's nice just holding it. Wonderful engineering. Everything moves so smoothly. Holding it is like holding a clock with the cover off. You know it's special and that it'll tell you things that you can't find out anywhere else, once you know how to use it.

It's really a triangle with a curved base, a quadrant. There's an arm which pivots at the top of the triangle. It has a viewfinder like a small telescope and lots of mirrors and shades so you can look at stars. All you're doing is measuring the angle between a star and the horizon from where you're standing.

You look through the sextant eyepiece and pick up the star in the viewer and the mirror, more or less as if you were looking at them through a telescope, which I suppose is what it is. Then you move the sextant arm down, and the image of the star comes with you. You do this until the star in the mirror just clips the horizon.

You know the angle because it's marked on the curved bit, the quadrant of the sextant. Then you have to nip into the chartroom – counting one-and-two-and-three and so on because you have to get an exact time, down to the second, from the chronometer. Why? Well, the Mate says that's because the stars are changing position all the time (rising and going down) and we've got almanacs that tell us exactly (I think) what an altitude should be at any time. Once you've got the altitude and the exact time you took it, then you do the sums with all the books and almanacs. These tell you what the angle should be, what other figures you have to use to adjust for that exact time on that exact day. From this, you get all the corrections to make. Get even three stars and you know where you are because it's just angles. The Mate says it's just like standing in a city. If you stand on a street corner and get all the angles between you and the edges of buildings, then the lines will cross where you're standing in relation to the buildings. It's a bit different when there's cloud, no horizon and the ship's rolling about all over the place. Still, it's better than chipping and scraping.

## 20 MARCH 1958, INDIAN OCEAN

More sextant on the four to eight with the Mate. We went through the stars and I got most of them. Ainslie says it's good for pulling girls. They like that sort of thing. I said there aren't any girls. He said I'd never get chance to try it because they'd never let me get near enough to tell them about my Big Dipper. He thought that was really funny. I didn't bother to laugh. Ainslie's not the Mate. Anyway, I was too busy trying to figure out my sextant.

The Mate took it upon himself to continue his role of housemaster-cum-tutor. There was no one else to do it, unless the Second Mate took an interest. There was nothing in his contract that said he should. Most times, the Second Mate knew exactly what his contract said. This one was a great sleeper. Loved his bunk.

## 21 MARCH 1958, OFF DONDRA HEAD

The Second Mate's always in his scratcher. I think he's trying to sleep through the whole voyage. I had to do the twelve to four with him this week. He said that he'd sailed in a Trinity House yacht for a long time. I asked him where. He looked at me for a long time. I think he thought I was being cheeky. He said, You don't go anywhere, only to things. Sounded daft. What sort of things? He said they went to the Isle of Wight for the yacht racing. There's a poster for trains to the Isle of Wight at Bexleyheath station. Haven't got one for Shanghai. I think I'd rather go to Shanghai. I said why did he leave the Trinity House ship. He just said he had reasons. I suppose we all have those. Ainslie said it was a woman. I said how did he know? He said it always is. Ainslie's got a girlfriend called Veronica and he's got her picture on the bulkhead, so perhaps he knows a thing or two about it. It would explain why the Second Mate is always in his bunk. Probably best to sleep if you don't want to think about something.

## 22 MARCH 1958, INDIAN OCEAN

On with the Second Mate again. Heading for Malacca Strait. He's a strange bloke. Sometimes he'll come out on to the wing of the bridge and chat. During the night you have to speak quietly because it'll wake the Captain. His night cabin's just below on the starboard side, and he has the ports open and you can hear everything at sea. So you can only really talk on the port side, which is where the Second Mate makes me go anyway. He doesn't like apprentices in the wheelhouse. Says they're no good as lookouts all cosy inside. He likes them to stay out on the wing of the bridge, especially if the weather's shitty. And he says, 'Don't forget to keep an eye astern, not just ahead. You never know what'll creep up your arse. One of the big tankers could be up you before you know where you are, and they never keep a proper lookout.' And he creeps about.

I was just dozing off when I heard a cough and he was nearly behind me. I started a sort of humming. I hope he thought I was awake. I mentioned it to Ainslie this morning and I said if he hadn't coughed I'd have been in for it. Ainslie wanted to know who was the stand-by quartermaster. I told him it was the one with the big sheath knife. I don't know the Chinese names yet. Thought so, he said. That was the cough. He was warning you. Does it for me. The Second Mate's a bastard like that. Then why did the quartermaster warn me? Well, says Ainslie, it's because the Second Mate makes the quartermaster get him lime juice and tea, and he thinks that's steward's work. Nice to know we have at least one friend on board.

The Second Mate was right about keeping a lookout. The sleep pattern wasn't hard, but for a youngster it took a lot of getting used to. Getting to sleep about nine in the evening if he were lucky, having to get up two and three-quarter hours later, at the very latest, and then being sharp-eyed and full of wits took plenty of adjustment for a young growing body. Hardly surprising that there were moments when daydreaming, even in the middle of the night, could be extremely dangerous. The Tramp was blind without its human lookouts. Other ships had whirring radar scanners, although how many were properly manned was another thing. Also, on some bridges the radar gave the mates a false sense of seamanship. The radar set saw everything. So it did, if the range was set properly. So it did, if it were properly read and the display properly acted on. The accountants in The Tramp's head office had a point. More than once radar had been an aid to collision instead of navigation. For the apprentice, however, the discussion was not so often about the art of technical navigation as above soogee-ing. Soogee-ing, cleaning the most obstinately dirty parts of a ship, could inspire the grumpiest reflections.

## 27 MARCH 1958, MALACCA STRAIT

I hate soogee-ing. Really, really, really hate it. I can't think why I do because it's not that important. It's a better job than chipping and scraping, but I hate it more. Mum says she hates ironing more than anything else – even cooking, which she really can't see the point of. Soogee-ing is worse than all the ironing in the world, to be done in one afternoon when the sun is shining for the only time that it ever will that summer. First thing you need is an old paint tin. Seems everything's an old paint tin. You look at a row of them in the fo'c's'le and not one of them has the same thing in. Shackles in one. Then nuts. Then bolts. Brushes. Old files that the casab's going to sharpen down as scrapers. Bits of rag. Even tea. I swear some of the Chinkies have tea in them. As far as I can see the best use for an old paint tin is cutting it down the middle and poking it through the porthole. Makes a brilliant vent. I wonder how it is that a paint tin is the same diameter as a porthole? You get plenty of time to think about that sort of thing when you're soogee-ing. Soogee-ing's washing and scrubbing things down.

I asked the Mate what language it is. He said Indian. The Second Mate said Chinese. I asked the casab and he just said, Me no understand this fashion – or something like that. So nobody knows. Something else to think about when you're doing it. Yesterday, we had to do all the midships accommodation's outside bulkheads. You get yet another paint tin with some liquid soap, which I think is the soogee itself, from the casab, and maybe some soda in it, but you don't have rags. Instead you get old bits of frayed mooring ropes. Dip and scrub. Dip and scrub. Five hours of dip and scrub. Today was worse. We had to do the lifeboat oars. Another paint tin. This time you put some sand in and a bit of sea water. You put the wet sand on old bits of canvas and scrub like buggery all morning. When that's done, you get old rope ends and rub the whole thing down. Job and finish, said the Mate. Took from eight this morning until six this evening. I bet people ashore would get overtime – and they'd have skin left on their hands. Then we get the bonus: we have to soogee all the deck where we've done the sand and canvassing.

## 28 March 1958, Pulu Bukum

Pulu Bukum for bunkers. The Mate says Singapore's the place. Still conrad, he says. When I got below, I asked Ainslie what a conrad was. He hasn't got a clue. Told me the Mate was probably taking the piss. He said that if the Mate told me to go and get one, I was just to say aye, aye, sir and do something else. I told the Third Engineer what Ainslie said. He said Ainslie was taking the mickey and leading me on. Apparently it's a bloke. Joseph Conrad. He wrote books about Singapore. I suspect the Third knows what he's talking about. He's Scotch and always reckons the schools are better up there. I think he's wrong about Ainslie. He didn't know. If he had done he'd have rubbed my nose in it. Always does. Never misses a chance.

Thought I'd try this Conrad out on the Mate. I asked him if he had any of his books. So you know who he is, he said. Oh yes, sir, I said. Wrote all about Singapore, didn't he? Not quite, Chuck, not quite, but it'll do for starters, he said. He told me to come and see him at the end of the watch. When I went down, he didn't say anything. Just handed me this book. It's called *Lord Jim*. Start there, he said.

The relationship between the apprentice and the Mate was sort of housemaster and boy. Maybe first-year sixth-former. The apprentice was trying to find his own way into adulthood, but there were few, if any, others doing the same thing. No peers. He was the youngest on the ship. So when he talked to anyone, with the exception of the one other apprentice, then he was talking to an adult. There were no street corners to hang around on, no one of his own age to mutter with, to plot with, to dream with. The sea wasn't a boy's world. It was, so they said, a man's world. So from day one he had to be a man. Grandfather had been right. He'd come back a man. He had to mind he did it well. It was the Mate's job to make the process as easy as possible. The Mate was always considered a toughie. Had to be, otherwise too many would take advantage. Discipline. Thoroughness. Slackness. Then the ship wouldn't work. At the same time, he had to go easy when the moment was right. A broken apprentice running ashore to escape unhappiness was no good to the Mate. Anyway, it wasn't fair. Above all, the Mate had to be fair – if not always fair, always understanding. They weren't all. This one was. A good Catholic.

The Mate said Ainslie told him that I kneel down and say my prayers. That's the problem with sharing a cabin. Everyone knows everything. The Mate says that he's told Ainslie to leave me alone and if I want to say prayers that's OK by him. He then said it might be better if I said them when I was in bed. I said, Thank you, sir, but I'm not sure what it's got to do with him. He's not that important. Ainslie asked me if I'm a Catholic or something weird like that. I said that I just liked doing it. Then I thought I could really get him going. So I said that if he liked I'd say some for him. He said he'd smack my head if I did. I said I might without telling him. He said then he'd smack my head without telling me. I don't think he's ever smacked anyone's head. He's really quite funny. I heard him last night telling the Third Engineer that he thinks I just say prayers to annoy him and because I want to be different. The Third didn't say anything for a bit, then in that quiet Scotch voice of his said that he sometimes said prayers, so what did that make him? I don't know what happened after that, but I bet Ainslie didn't tell him he was going to smack his head.

The Tramp, having bunkered in Pulu Bukum, now sailed further east for Korea. Korea was sort of tagged on to China. He knew nothing more than that until he went to his atlas and the ship's charts. Curiously, he sensed he knew more about Korea, because of the recent war. It had been over only five years. Finished in coronation year. He knew a lot about that. The Queen, Everest and Korea. The death of Stalin had not been brought to his attention. Some people had bought televisions that year, 1953, for the coronation. His parents hadn't and so they'd gathered that June day in a friend's front room. Curtains drawn against the sunlight, ham sandwiches cut and wrapped in greaseproof paper. He'd never seen television again, and Korea hadn't been mentioned anyway. Yet he had vague memories from the Pathe Pictorial Newsreels before the B-film at the Erith Odeon.

## 10 APRIL 1958, KUNSAN

According to the Fourth, Korea's older than England. Can't be. Oh yes it can, he said. England's only been England for a thousand years. Korea's been here since 666. How did he remember that? Because it's magic numbering, he said. That's right. Auntie Heron's sister's a witch. Dad says she told him that Mr Woodcock's car was unlucky because it had 666 on the numberplate. The next week, Mr Woodcock crashed into the river. Dad said it was because he'd been in the Fox and Hounds since opening time, but Mum said it was 666. I wonder if the Koreans think it's unlucky. Maybe that's why they lost the war.

## 13 APRIL 1958

This is South Korea. I had a run ashore. It's pretty grim: mostly mud streets, and the houses are not much more than huts. I found some old bloke selling paintings. I've bought one. It's only small and is mainly blue. It's a small lake with a black boat, probably a skiff, on it. I was wondering what to do next because I hadn't got any more money when I met these two American airmen. They said they're here all the time. They are at the air base. I asked them if they'd been in the war. No, sir, they said.

They'd been drafted. That sounds the same as National Service. I've never met an American before. They're quite big. One of them said he liked the picture and that he thought the man who painted it had no hands. Held the brush in his toes. When I got back I told Ainslie. He said if I believed that I'd believe anything. I suppose I would. Who cares? I've got plenty of time to make up my mind about almost everything.

# 7

## CATHAY AND SEX

Only part of the cargo was bound for Korea; the rest was to go to Japan. The run from Kunsan to Osaka was three days or so. An easy passage along the western seaboard of Kyushu. Sailed by Nagasaki. The name meant nothing. Although, he'd been born then, few understood the magnitude of anything but the nuclear mushroom. Then along the southern coast of Shikoku and into the tight bay, almost a lagoon on the chart, of Hokkaido and then Osaka. Three days from Kunsan. A decade in industrial time.

### 17 APRIL 1958, OSAKA

Anchored off Osaka last night. I was on anchor-watch, just keeping a general eye and checking bearings to make sure we weren't dragging. I couldn't see much until first light, then it was just like one of those Japanese paintings. The water's completely still, and as the sun came up all the other ships and boats were blodges, not sharp enough to be silhouettes, just blodges against the yellowy-brown (I think that's the colour) mist. Ainslie came up to the bridge and I said wasn't it an amazing colour. It's shit, he said. He's really got a way with words. I said I thought it was beautiful. You would, he said. That's because you know sod all about sod all. It's yellow because it's sulphur from the sodding factories. Forget the fancy toe painting or *Madame Butterfly* crap. It's part of their wonderful industrial revolution. They chuck all the industrial waste into the air or the sea. I said it was just like London and smogs. He said everyone was the same. Didn't matter where you went. You had a sodding great world war. Killed as many people as you could and then tried to kill the rest with progress coming out of chimneys instead of gun barrels. I asked him what he was going to do about it. He said if Mr Churchill couldn't care a toss why should he. Just remember two things, he said. Don't drink the water and always remember to wash your willy after you've shagged their women.

Ainslie is strange. He comes out with something as strong as the thing about smoke and philosophy and then somehow spoils it by saying things like that. Somewhere deep down he's very angry. I wish he liked me, then I could ask him why.

## 18 APRIL 1958, OSAKA

This sex thing is pretty tricky. Everyone seems to know so much about it. Some of them go ashore just to do it. We go to a bar, sit around having a few beers and then it's 'who's got change for ten dollars?' and they're off. It's not that I feel left out. No one says you have to, except the Second Mate. He said that a lad of my age ought to be getting his end away. Can't keep it to stir your tea with, he said.

The Third Engineer heard him. He said, Don't worry. The Third never bags off. Never. He has a picture of his wife on his desk and says goodnight to her every night. About one o'clock this morning we were outside a bar where the noodle man comes. He turns up on his bicycle just like the ice-cream man outside school. While we were waiting, the Third was telling me about his home in Montrose. It sounds sort of very proper. I don't mean all churchy proper. Just ordinary. He's the only one who talks about his family. His wife sounds really nice. I told him that I didn't know much about sex. At school the sex education lessons were done in biology and I didn't do biology. Then there wasn't much going on at the youth club. I suppose there might have been, but I didn't know about it. He wanted to know if I had a girlfriend. No. Never? No. He said, You must have had a girlfriend of some sort. No. We were just a crowd, and because I don't have brothers and sisters then I never really talked about things like that. He said there was plenty of time. For what? For looking back, he said. I don't know what he means, but it's nice to have someone you can go ashore with just for a beer and a look around.

From Osaka to Hong Kong. Even then, there was a sense that China was waiting. A sense that, should they choose, they would simply walk across the border and take what they believed rightfully theirs. In those days, Britain's colonial writ was being torn up in front of their faces. The formality of the treaty that would in some forty years give up to China the island and mainland territories might not be enough for Peking, as then it was, to be happy with a promise.

In the late 1950s China had two images for a lad brought up in a Kentish village. They were small people – and there were millions of them – who wore pigtails and they had rickshaws instead of bikes. As no one in his family had ever had a car, he thought push-bikes and rickshaws a fair comparison. He had a vague idea about Chinese Communism, but he'd never heard of Mao Tse-tung. There were Chinese in the East End of London. He knew that. Never seen them, but he'd been told. They lived behind dark doors off dim alleyways. He didn't know about Chinese cooking. Apart from fish-and-chip shops, takeaways had not been invented in the 1950s, not in his bit of Kent. There was a Wimpy Bar in Bexleyheath Broadway, and that was about as exciting as it got in that town. When from the barge hatchway he'd seen a Chinaman staring down from the deck of a freighter he'd been a little frightened. It was the first he'd seen. On the first morning, when the lad joined The Tramp, he'd walked along the gangway looking for his cabin. Coming towards him was a Chinese deckhand. The lad had been nervous. His young mind wondered about a knife. He'd smiled – big and brave he was, as his aunt said he should be – and said hello. The deckhand said something he didn't catch. It had been all right after that. Within a week he laughed with the stewards, kept clear of the bosun and was friends with the chippie, the carpenter. So he knew a little about Hong Kong but was still uncertain as to what lay beyond the New Territories. Peking and Shanghai he understood were important, yet he didn't know where they were. Nanking he supposed was Chinese. Foochow was a mysterious place from where the chippie's father had come and where now his ashes rested. He heard from the Fourth how the war in Korea had started in 1950, and then he remembered names he'd heard his father and grandfather talk about. The battle of the Imjin River. The Glorious Gloucesters. Colonel Carn, VC – he thought that was the name, but the VC was right enough. He'd held out for days against all odds.

'They' hadn't been able to kill him. A living VC. He was a little confused about the difference between Korea and China. They all looked the same.

The lad knew nothing of the history of this vast land. Why should he? It had never been British and his classroom was mostly a shrine to his nation's history. He'd picked up bits and pieces. His Great-Uncle Eric had talked about the *Arrow* incident, 'when Victoria was on the throne'. Great-Uncle Eric had been in the navy 'when Victoria was on the throne' – just. Certainly not between 1856 and 1860, when Britain was fighting to hang on to what she, and the French for that matter, regarded as rights to trade in China. There were agreements, documents signed. But who signed? Who agreed? It was a mysterious country. They really did have pigtails. There were sleeves to hide hands. One day, in October 1856, Chinese officials boarded and arrested a small vessel called the *Arrow*, then threw her crew into prison. The vessel – 'ship' is too grand a name – had a British name, but it was owned by a Chinaman. He lived in Hong Kong, so the *Arrow* was a colonial vessel, non-Chinese. The French, who, as always, had their own agenda, joined forces with the British. This was war. The French and the British won, but not before the Chinese had broken truces, committed outrages and had, for their pains of course, the sacred Summer Palace in the forbidden city, Peking, burned down. The British and French demanded the right to set up their embassies in Peking, a place in which no foreigners were allowed to live. And the Opium Wars? The Chinese tried to stop British merchants smuggling opium and refused to pay compensation for doing so. The British, of course, won. That was in 1842. Having won, there had to be a treaty and the Chinese had to pay. The price, in that Treaty of Nanking, was Hong Kong. That was how Britain got it. The lad didn't know this. But the Fourth did and told him.

## 30 April 1958, Hong Kong

It's Mum's birthday today. I wish I'd sent a card. I was going to from Japan. Couldn't see any. Now she'll think I haven't bothered. I've written. I was going to leave it until I'd seen Hong Kong. Instead I've told her and Dad about Korea and Japan. It's difficult to write a letter about something you think the person wasn't expecting. I told them about the mud in Korea and lots of building in Japan. Before I got there I thought I would be writing about something else. I'm not sure what. Teahouses and kimonos, I suppose. They're there. But what's there more than anything else is movement. The whole of Osaka was moving. The people were all going in different directions but looking as if they were going somewhere. No one was standing around talking. Everyone seemed to have somewhere to go. Most of the buildings looked as if they weren't very strong and they were mostly scruffy. But the people in them looked very clean. The Fourth says that when they have a bath, they wash before they get in. Why? Because they'd be rinsing in dirty water, wouldn't they? I said I suppose they would. No suppose about it, he said, they would. He's right. Why haven't we thought of that? Mum loves lying in the bath for ages. She's just lying in dirty water then. We get into Hong Kong in about three hours. This, says everyone, is the place to come to. Everyone looks forward to it. Everything's very cheap and there's a lot of it. That sounds all right.

For The Tramp's stewards, deckhands and greasers, Hong Kong was home. Sign off. Sign on again. Most of them would. Another two years. They didn't mind. By now, the lad was getting to know them. Even the bosun smiled at him. Or was he laughing? The chippie was teaching him Cantonese. Friends. So the run ashore in the colony was special. A visit to Ah Ping's flat. Small. Neat. Tiny, gold-toothed wife. So many children. Five, not four. Very important. Four was a bad Chinese number.

To the lad, Hong Kong was the place he'd always wanted to go to. It was the furthest place he could ever imagine. Australia may have been further away for all he knew, but it didn't seem so. It wasn't foreign. Just Australia. It was Hong Kong they talked about at home. It's ours. Still an outpost. A proper colony. The picture books said it conformed to everything he'd been taught. The Chinese knew their place; more important, so did he. He could see colonialism for himself. Proper British colonialism. Everyone, including the locals, proper British in sunshine and shorts.

The Shaukiwan tram was open-topped, but it was the same as the one his dad had driven from Abbey Wood to New Cross, although there was no need for the foot button that dropped sand on to the lines when the frost bit. The policemen were Chinese in khaki and black caps, dressed by the colonial tailor. Always a British inspector in charge. Shorts, long socks and heat rashes. The Coca-Cola bottling plant on the outskirts of Taikoo showed the place was up to date. It was nearly as important as having a Co-op. In Victoria, the centre of Hong Kong island, there was still a cricket ground, branches of Bond Street shops, familiar names from his imperial history lessons, and, of course, Chinese tailors and watch shops. A Tissot for £8, an Omega for £20. He'd never had a watch. Now he had a Tissot. He'd wear it for the rest of his life just as he'd wear the memory of that suit. The Suit. The First Suit.

# 1 May 1958, Hong Kong

I have a suit. Or I will have tomorrow. The first suit in my whole life. Ainslie can't believe it. I wasn't going to tell him, but it slipped out. He said it was a wonder I had any shoes, and with a name like mine I was probably a Gypsy and my dad was probably sharpening knives. I didn't take any notice. When I asked him where I should go, he said all the expensive tailors were too good for me. He said, Come with me. Last night he took me to the Flying Angel down by the harbour. It's an amazing place, a sort of big hostel for sailors from everywhere. Not the normal Flying Angel. It's the biggest in the world. Big as the biggest hotel. Must be. In one corner there are two rooms. This is the tailor. Open all night. Meakers in Bexleyheath close at five and half-day closing is Thursday, and they're the best. I told Ainslie this, and he said these people make Meakers look like the Co-op. I nearly said, What's wrong with the Co-op? but on some things Ainslie is right. I suppose I don't know very much about some of the things he does. This tailor is amazing. You don't go in and find something that nearly fits, like Dad did for John and Tilda's wedding. They actually measure you and make it to fit. Ainslie says it's called bespoke tailoring. I said, What does bespoke mean? He said, Made to measure. I said, I know that, but what does the word 'bespoke' mean? He said, No one knows. In other words, he doesn't know. There's a big sign: MADE TO MEASURE 48 HOURS. And it only costs £12. I spent two hours going through the pattern book. Ainslie said, Get grey, three buttons and nothing fancy. That's what he did. But then that's what he is. I've got a brown and black stripe. Three buttons and an extra side pocket. The tailor said it was a ticket pocket. I asked him what sort of ticket. Ainslie said, Bus ticket and it's the only one you'll ever get. He thought that was really funny, but then had to explain to the tailor that a ticket was what we call the Second Mates' Certificates of Competency. It didn't sound so funny when he had to explain. But that didn't stop him telling the whole ship when we got back. And I've got a pair of shoes. This place makes you a pair for £4. They're going to be the same sort of brown as the suit. I have to go back tonight at about eleven to make sure everything fits and then pick it all up tomorrow. I've written to Mum to tell her. She won't believe it. She works in Hedley Mitchells in Erith, and I remember she once said that Mr Mitchell was a real toff and had his suits made for him in London. Bet he never had one done in the Flying Angel in Hong Kong. I wonder what she'll think?

## 2 MAY 1958, HONG KONG

I've got a broken nose. Ainslie had a Dear John today. His girlfriend's chucked him. Says she's marrying a bloke who works in Boots. I said I thought only women worked in Boots and, anyway, if she's doing that she can't be up to much. He said that she'd said that he couldn't expect her to be pure while he was away for two years. Not at her age. I said, That just proves what I said. She must be putting it about. Just think what would have happened if you'd married her. He didn't say much and left. I thought I'd put it nicely and cheered him up. About half an hour later he came back. Said he'd been thinking what I'd said about Veronica and that I was a dirty-minded little turd and he punched me in the face. Blood everywhere. So's my nose.

## 3 MAY 1958, HONG KONG

The Mate's put me in the book for fighting. Stopped my shore leave. Ainslie said sorry. He thinks I was right after all. Said I look better with a broken nose and thinks I'll be able to pull more birds. Thanks very much, I said. Pity I can't get ashore to find out.

## 4 MAY 1958, HONG KONG

Shore leave on again so I've got the suit. I think it looks good. The Third said he thought the brown and black stripes were a bit bold. Sort of thing band leaders wear, he said. I said I thought they all wore blazers. Only the best ones, he said.

PS The nose isn't broken. But it's bent. I'm not sure what the difference is.

## 6 MAY 1958

Had a run ashore in Wanchai last night. Thought about wearing the suit, but I wasn't sure what might happen so I left it in the locker. Everyone in the Cherry Bar seemed to know Ainslie, especially some tiny Chinese girl who says her name's Rose (I bet) with her skirt slit up to her armpits. She was all over him. Personally, I didn't think much of her. Really chunky and her fingers were dirty. A friend of hers came over. She was quite pretty. Nice smile. Quiet, not like her friend, who by now was sitting on Ainslie's lap and bouncing up and down. Ainslie said I had to buy the girl a drink. They're drinking some green stuff in small glasses like Nanna takes every night for her belly. I said why should I? They wanted $4 for the stuff, which I reckon was just coloured water. I said $4 was about 7/6d. I said you could buy a crate of the stuff for 7/6d in a shop. He said not to be so sodding mean. Then his Rose said, You buy drink, she do very good jiggy-jig. That's right, said Ainslie, get your end away; don't be mean. I'm beginning to take Veronica's side. Personally, I didn't think much of his girl. The quiet one's OK except she kept saying, You chelly boy? Ainslie thought this was very funny. He said maybe I'd get my end away for nothing if I said I was cherry. So he told the whole bar I was. The one who was with me wanted to know how old I am. I said seventeen. And you still chelly boy? That velly good. Anyone would think I'd said I played centre forward for Charlton.

Except for Rose, they all say their name's Suzie Wong. I can't see why they're supposed to be good-looking. They're really titchy and they've got crackly voices. I suppose that's because they're noisy. None of this mysterious eastern stuff I read about. But it was good fun. Bit different from the youth club at All Saints Church. Don't think the Reverend Maxwell would like this.

There was a lumpy American sailor from a ship called the *Chuck R. Berry*. He wanted to know if I knew the Queen or any of her family. I told him about the street party we had for the coronation five years ago. He said, Did you get to sit next to her? I said, Where? At the party. Not exactly, I said. We made do with a photograph, but it was quite good because Mr Coleman had made a gold frame for it. He looked disappointed, so I said I'd met Mr Churchill, which was sort of true. He'd never heard of Mr Churchill, which is a bit odd considering that he spoke English.

He's asked me if I'd like to come and see his ship. He thinks it might be possible as I'm English. I think I'll go. Ainslie said later that I'd better watch my backside. All these Americans are like that. I said if he was a queer how come he was in the bar with the Suzie Wongs? Ainslie said that didn't mean anything and if I went to the warship I should take him with me. He's not very subtle. Anyway, that was last night.

I came back to the ship by myself. Ainslie said he was bagging off. He came back on board at about three this morning. Made a racket getting into his bunk. He had a big plaster over his eye and his lip's split. He said that after I left the Yank had tried to bag off with Rose, or whatever her name was. I said, I thought you said he was a woofter. As usual, he threatened to smack me one, but his heart wasn't in it. I'm beginning to think Ainslie doesn't have much luck with girls.

The dockyard work was done by Hong Kong Chinese – 'dockyard mateys', as they were called. Over in Kowloon, where the Royal Navy docked, Hong Kong Mary ruled. She ran the biggest and toughest Mrs Mop organisation in the British Empire. The colony was labour-intensive, and for the sailors the most remarkable sight was hundreds of Hong Kong Mary's women in black 'pyjamas' waiting on the dry-dock wall. Same over at Taikoo, where the old trading company of Swires ruled.

The Tramp, more than 7,000 tons and 425 feet of steel, was gently nudged to the mouth of the dock. Like some gentle pagan rite, the vessel would be coaxed between the stone limbs until settled fore and aft and made fast to steel bollards and bits. Behind her, the gates would be closing even as her stern lines were ashore. When tight shut, the dock water emptied as fast as a Friday night bath. Silently watching, the army of mateys. The Tramp was hardly settled and dock walls still wet, and up would go the bamboo poles, crisscrossed and tied with raffia. This was the wonkiest scaffold in the world. But they could (and did) set it to build skyscrapers. As the poles went up, so cone-hatted ants swarmed. Each wore a face mask and was heavily armed with a sharp-edged chipping hammer and scraper – a tool like a big rasp file that had been ground to a sharp blade at its toe end. Within minutes, the irritable symphony of chipping hammers would start until there wasn't a square inch of the hull that hadn't been stripped to the steel. That done, gallon after gallon of red lead was slopped on, then black topsides, and for a moment she'd be as spruce as a Jardine flagship.

The Taikoo Dock was at Quarry Bay, between North Point and Shaukiwan. Once they'd built fine ships in that dock. Not any more. The *Hunan* would be built there in 1969, but it was a one-off. The real business was to be done in repairing passing trade, a sort of crown colony maritime garage. That dockyard was almost a colony within a colony. Hardly the Tyne, the Wear, the Clyde. Lawns, bowling green, swimming pool. A low building that was the officers' mess for the Mates and engineers who sailed the China Navigation Company ships. The CN Co. bungalow they called it. Alongside was the famous Taikoo Club, a modernish building built to preserve the old ways with considerable comfort. A senior common room for expatriates. A Scot with a black military moustache (there were seemingly more Scots than any others, although not all with moustaches) was to be found regularly with a whisky and lemonade and an equally distinctive mix of metaphors to describe what he believed to be the decline of the colony and British rule throughout the known world – known that is, to expatriates, who everyone had to understand 'kept the show on the road'. Hong Kong would remain British for more than thirty years more. The treaty would expire in 1997 and then, of course, the place would go 'to hell in a hand basket'. There was a grass bank by the front of the club. Very green. The one with the moustache said it reminded him of 'back home'. But really, this was his home. The colonies were their real homes. Send them back to the UK and most of them hadn't much. They'd make something of it when the time came – a bungalow somewhere; Bexhill-on-Sea was always favoured – but they'd not be much without their houseboys, armahs, dhobi wallahs and that tin of fifty Players and a bottle of Gordon's, all for less than a pound. A pound could cure a lot of homesickness.

## 7 MAY 1958, HONG KONG

The Third Mate is quite friendly. He keeps asking me if I'm homesick and that if I am then not to worry. He said the best thing is to write home. I said that that makes it worse. He said I'm writing the wrong things. He said don't keep asking how everyone is. Don't ask if the dog's still alive. Don't keep giving your love to everybody. He said, All you're doing is thinking about it, and it's always much better than it really was when you're thinking about it 11,000 miles away. Anyway, he said, it's daft asking questions in letters. It's not like a telephone. You can't hear the answers. He said the best thing to do is tell them about you and the ship and everything you've been doing – or almost everything. That's what they want to hear and, he said, when you tell them what you're doing, then you stop feeling homesick because it makes you realise that this is better than anything they've got and it's why you're here. He may be right.

There were moments, walking up and down the windward wing of the bridge on the midnight to four watch, when he thought of home.

But not much. He hadn't much to think about. Nothing to long for.

## 7 MAY 1958, TAIKOO DOCK

I quite missed the cat. Proper cat. Ginger. But that's about it. I feel a bit guilty about not missing Mum and Dad. I do really, but then I don't. I like Dad, but I can't say I miss him. Same with Mum. I suppose because I know they're there. If they weren't there, then I'd miss them. Another thing: I'm not ready to show them that I've really done anything. I don't feel different yet. If I saw them now, they wouldn't see any difference. Just think I've been out for a bit. Mum probably thinks the same thing. I've had a couple of airmails from her. But she doesn't say very much. The writing's quite spaced out. Said they'd been to Dymchurch. I don't feel homesick about Dymchurch. No one would feel that homesick. The other thing is that I'm lucky, not like Ainslie. I don't have to worry about having some girlfriend who might be going out with someone else.

It never dawned on him that while he daydreamed on the bridge, others paced their own emotions.

The Third Engineer deep below in his white boiler suit thinking about the beautiful wife he'd left in Montrose. Watching the huge and polished triple pistons going up and down, up and down, he'd be wondering what she was doing. Another cigarette and another read of the last letter he always kept in his boiler suit top pocket. The envelope was smudged from an oily thumb, but no archivist ever handled so delicately a priceless page of Sanskrit. But the lad wouldn't know that. No one in his family wrote those sort of letters.

The others? Maybe the skipper did think of home. Who could

possibly know what he thought? He gave nothing away. The Mate spoke of Ireland with a fondness that would have had him singing, although he'd never known how. He had a mother somewhere. Dundalk? Probably. The wireless operator kept his secret under his black eyebrows. You never knew if he was including you in a wink or he was overtired. But he never mentioned home. Few of them did. None was an aristocrat, so none knew another's family. Nothing in common that they'd talk about. Strange people with no lives ashore they were willing to share. Every few weeks they would steam into another port, as different as anything from the one they'd left. So nothing stayed the same for them to get used to one place. Nowhere looked like the places where they'd left their wives and gardens. So no reminders.

Their home was The Tramp and they took that with them. So no homesickness. Maybe it was why they always said that this would be their last trip and why they always came back. Couldn't settle, they'd say. Homesick, they meant.

## 8 May 1958, Hong Kong

Really strange yesterday. I was in the dockyard just wandering about because it's Saturday when I saw a boy called Ericson. He was at school with me. Well, not exactly because he was two years above me, except I kept wicket in the school First XI (two years early, hum hum) and he opened the batting. I didn't really know him, but out here it was like meeting a brother or something. He's going to university to be an engineer and he's having a holiday, staying with his uncle who's something important in the dockyard. We had a few beers and then his uncle turned up and said I could come to lunch with them.

It was strange going into someone's home. I'd more or less forgotten about being in some place where everything belonged just to one family. I'd forgotten about things lying about that belong to other people. I don't mean ornaments but personal things. There was someone's book open on the arm of a chair, and I didn't want to sit in the chair because the book had sort of bagged it. I wanted to have a look to see what these sort of people read, but I thought that would be rude. I went to the bathroom and there was some cotton thing hanging on the door. I suppose it's Erricson's aunt's or his cousin's, who's back in England at school, and I was really embarrassed. When I went back I felt his aunt was looking at me to see if I was red. I think I must have been, but that's daft. Then there was a desk in the room and it had photographs on it. They weren't just faces like most people have. There were pictures of people doing things. Sitting on a rug having sandwiches and tea. Another one on a beach. There was one of a really pretty girl on a horse. All the photographs were of a family doing things and different members of it being really happy. I think I felt I shouldn't be looking at other people, and their lives are private. I've never thought about it before. The only pictures we have out at home are of dead people. I thought that was why they're there. And just their faces. There's Great-Uncle Will in uniform before he was killed. There's one of Granddad Jim, and he's dead. Drowned at sea, Mum said. Drowned in whisky said Auntie Eva. Now she's dead I suppose they'll put her on the mantelpiece. On board you've got your cabin, or a bit of it, so you never have anything.

Ainslie says it's daft putting out things from home because that's only somewhere you go back to. He says when you go home on leave the first thing they ask you is when you're going back. But it was still strange being somewhere that they'll still be when we've gone.

I suppose I haven't really been in many different houses. Just my gran's and my aunts' and I've never been in anything like this. He must be a millionaire. He seems to have a lot of servants. It was a bit scary. Every time I moved, one of them was waiting to see what I wanted. His uncle smokes like a chimney, and when the ash gets about a quarter of an inch long there's one of these Chinkies with the ashtray. He keeps talking about people called expats. Seems they're the British who live here. He says most of them are here because they'd be pushed to get a decent job at home and they play, what he calls, the old colonial hand. He talked about the locals in a real nasty way. But the servants were there in the room when he said things – it's as if they don't actually see the servants. They're not there. I suppose you learn to do that when you're one of these colonial hands. Erricson said he'd thought of staying here instead of going to university and getting a job in the Hong Kong police. He says they'd make you a sub-inspector straight away because you were white. His uncle says there is a lot of corruption but that's the only way to keep crime at an acceptable level. I wanted to ask him how any crime could be acceptable. But I thought that wasn't too smart.

Erricson's aunt is really strange too. She's quite pretty. Erricson says she must be forty. It was very strange talking to a lady I didn't know. I don't think I've ever done that before. I've never really had to speak to ladies except Mum and the family. I suppose there was the vicar's wife, but she never said much except to make sure I wiped my feet. Then I suppose there were the teachers at school. Mrs Mountley was the only one I really knew. She was the French teacher and said I could be good at it if I put my mind to it. I suppose Ericson's aunt is a bit like talking to a teacher. You have to put your mind to it and be polite, but there's not much to say. She started asking if I knew lots of people in Kent. I hadn't heard of any of them. She said she supposed that those people had been away at school. Billy Butler on the barge used to say he'd been away at school, but he meant borstal. Don't think she meant that.

## 10 MAY 1958, AT SEA

I wasn't going to say anything about this, but I've been thinking about it. It's about Ericson's aunt and what he's told me makes it easier to write this down. When we'd had lunch she said I had to see the view. She said you could see China. I said that I thought this was China. Well, sort of, and anyway, didn't we have to give it back? That didn't do me much good. We went on to the balcony and next thing she's rubbing her hand on my trousers. Mrs Mountley never did that. Anyway, I have to say that I was quite frightened. I thought of saying I was going to be sick, but that would have been a bit dramatic. Then I thought it was no good saying I had to go to the khazi, because I'd just been and, anyway, she might have got the wrong impression. What really frightened me was what would happen if Ericson's uncle came out. She didn't say anything about it. She just kept talking about the sodding view and kept rubbing. Then she just wandered off, and the next thing I started saying I had to be back on board.

Ericson came on board this morning and he said he'd seen her trying to get her hand down my trousers, but not to worry, his uncle didn't see, and anyway, she's doing it all the time. He said she hasn't worn knickers since she was thirteen. Then he said they're going to Sheiko Beach for a picnic and I was invited. I said I had to keep ship for the next couple of days so couldn't go.

I'm glad we're back at sea. It's safer.

We're going to America to load timber for Australia. If we go to Sydney, I can see Auntie Joyce and Uncle Eric.

# 8

---

# THE WORLD TURNED UPSIDE DOWN

The west coast of America presented a problem. He only believed in New York.

This, remember, was the 1950s. Images didn't get too jumbled. No channel-hopping in those days. No channels. His image of America began with food parcels sent by a distant uncle in New Jersey who'd heard about rationing and starvation in the old country. Cookies. Hershey bars. Comic sections from fat newspapers. When the distant uncle came to see for himself, it was the zigzag of purples, yellows and greens of his kipper tie that stuck in the lad's imagination. Then came Bill Haley and the Comets, Elvis, Little Richard and a belief that a dollar bill was really exciting.

At eleven, he'd been given one by the uncle. Still had it. Would always have it. Dollar. How much is that? Dollar quarter. Quarter. Two bits. Dime. Nickel. Exciting words. People with dollars and a piece of change were exciting. They didn't have dollars on the Belvedere marshes. Had very little, really. Even their chewing gum came in penny packets of pellets from yellow machines bolted to Derrett and Dorman's shop wall.

No one chewed gum like an American. They chewed not on boring pavements but on sidewalks. No boring trams. Streetcars. The subway. 'Little boids sitting on da koib eatin' da dirty woims,' said the uncle. And made them laugh. In New York, he said, the skyscrapers were the biggest in the world. Chevvies had big fins. Caddies had millionaires. Shallow? Yes, of course. Which was why the images were so strong. But what lay beyond the Bronx and Manhattan? He didn't know. He knew all about Kit Carson, Wyatt Earp, General Custer. He didn't know that Carson City existed. That Dodge City was real. Had a mayor, high schools, sidewalks and dollar bills. He'd never much believed the Saturday morning pictures at the Odeon. So he dismissed the rest of America as being an illusion. New York wasn't an illusion. Everyone knew that.

You could draw New York. You couldn't draw anywhere else in America.

Now he heard the Second Engineer talking about 'Frisco as if it were his backyard. Maybe once it was. The Third Mate had an Ivy League second cousin by marriage with a law firm in Los Angeles. Of course he had. But they weren't going to San Francisco. Certainly not LA. They were loading timber. Timber from Small Town, USA. Make the first landfall off Cape Disappointment and then into Astoria, just across the river from Washington State, so in Oregon. Lines of railroad trucks. Georgia Pacific Lumber. Sounded a lot better than Thorn's Wood Yard (Bexleyheath) Ltd. Then down to Coos Bay and North Bend, then further south into Eureka, California. No surfin'. Just a jukebox playing 'To Know Him Is to Love Him' while he waited for his shoe to be fixed, and there was a man who'd worked on the buses in Woolwich.

## 7 JUNE 1958, ASTORIA

It's quite cold here. The wharfies wear really good warm clothes. Proper lumberjack coats. Red and black tartan and black sheepskin hats with ear covers. They're very big. All of them. Even when they're not tall, they're very broad. Each one carries a big cargo hook with an amazingly sharp point. When the timber swings inboard it sometimes needs stacking, and they'll slam the point of their cargo hook into it as if the wood was as soft as a jelly baby. Imagine them using one of those in a fight, said the Second Mate. Over on the east coast, they do, said the Mate. They're nice people here. Nice voices. Very deep. Like cowboys. That sounds daft now, but it's true. They work for Georgia Pacific Lumber and do this all the time. One of them was telling me that Oregon and Washington State, which is on the other side of the Snake River from us (or is it the Astoria River? I'll have to check), are the best places to live in the whole United States. I said what about New York? He said, That's not America, that's New York. He said that Oregon was clean and the people easy-going. That seems right. The bread's wonderful. It's good to get fresh milk and bread. On board we have it for about three days after leaving port, then we have to use the powdered stuff and the bread the cook makes, which is OK but not brilliant. This American bread is better than we get at home. It's very white and soft tasting. One thing that isn't good is I can't go in bars. Not old enough. You have to be twenty-one everywhere in America except for, I think, New Orleans. The Mate says they don't have any rules in New Orleans. Can't wait to get there. Love to take my trumpet and get to play in a gutbucket six. Just think, playing 'Basin Street Blues' in Basin Street. Not this trip. Ainslie said that he wouldn't bet on it. He never believes anyone knows for sure where we're going next until we tie up alongside. The Mate said that he was on one trip when they loaded scrap in Galveston for Kobe, then got orders halfway across the Pacific to take it to Shanghai and ended up unloading in Mojiko. Someone charters, sells the cargo during the voyage, the new owner's got a better customer and the rate's fixed in somewhere like London and they all go home with cigars. Next morning we get a message to say turn right for Waikikakow or somewhere. So the Mate says, anyway.

## 8 JUNE 1958, ASTORIA

Ainslie's had a letter from Veronica. She says she's not getting married to the bloke in Boots after all. Ainslie said he knew she wouldn't. She says she can't wait until he's home. Seems to be that was what it was all about last time, she couldn't wait. I wouldn't bother to frame the letter and kiss it goodnight. Didn't tell him that.

One of the quartermasters is very sharp. He's also very stupid. He was on gangway-duty this evening. The Americans put one of their own guards on the gangway as well. I'm not quite sure why. But they do. Anyway, the guard has got a big wristwatch with knobs and switches sticking out the sides and so many dials you can hardly see the watch bit. It can, he says, give you the time anywhere in the world – even fry eggs to order for all I know. Suddenly, the little quartermaster, who is one of life's showoffs, said he thought the guard's watch was crap. The guard looks like an advertisement for the state highway patrol, with every gadget and weapon known to man hanging from his belt. He took this insult quite badly. It got worse when the quartermaster said that, like everything else in America, the guard's watch looked good but had no guts. The guard just stared at him with his mouth open. He could not believe what he was hearing. The quartermaster, who, as I say, is mighty cocky, looked around and with a bit of a swagger took off his own watch, shoved it under the guard's nose and said, 'This, my flend, is man's watch. Best in world. It Lorex. You dive bottom of ocean and water no come in.'

'Don't get much call for that kinda thing,' said the guard.

The quartermaster started slapping his palm with the Rolex. 'This watch for big man. It no break.'

'That right?' said the guard. 'Guess every watch can break if you give it a hard time.'

The quartermaster looked really serious. 'I show you,' he said. 'I thlow this watch on deck. It no blake.'

'You don't say?' said the guard.

The quartermaster started waggling his watch at the guard again. 'We thlow watches on deck, then we see which one best watch.'

The guard looked at his wrist, then at the quartermaster's Rolex. He unstrapped his watch and then said to the quartermaster, 'OK, son. You got a deal. You first.'

And the dumb fool did! The quartermaster hurled it at the deck and it smashed.

The guard put his watch back on, smiling a little. 'Guess you lose, son,' he said, 'guess you lose.'

# 10 June 1958, North Bend

We stood off Coos Bay last night, waiting to come in. I was on bridge-watches with the Second Mate, and he had me taking bearings every fifteen minutes to fix our position. He said the coast here is tricky, and if we get it wrong then he'll be looking in the classified ads to buy a Welsh chicken farm. I said I thought they only had sheep in Wales. He said that nothing's easy.

I was watching the shoreside lights as well as the ones marked on the chart. Gives me an odd feeling. I suppose it's because the lights are about ordinary people doing ordinary things. We were close enough to see car lights and houses through binoculars. I started wondering who lived in the houses. Waiting off the coast in the dark and watching people being normal is a bit like being somebody from Mars in a spaceship. On board, we're all doing something. We all have jobs. The reason we're here is not because we're jolly jack tars and like the life. The company doesn't say go off to sea and enjoy yourselves and, by the way, while you're there would you mind delivering 9,000 tons of sugar or something to a bunch of people in Korea. We're here because someone in Korea always wants sugar, or whatever it is. But we're more like Martians than, say, Uncle Eddie, who might drive a tram and then give it back at night and go home, then come back in the morning and do it again. He goes home, has his tea, reads the paper, listens to *Ray's A Laugh* and then goes to bed. That's normal. We don't go home. I suppose we do because this is home. Come to think of it, when I was looking at the lights I started to think like someone in a flying saucer watching people who couldn't see me and who were different. I know a bit about them, and I know they speak English. I know they don't know how to eat with a knife and fork and that they drive on the other side of the road. They don't have kings and queens but they have film stars. Their cars are the biggest and they have skyscrapers. But that's about all I really know. I was up on the monkey island taking a bearing through the azimuth mirror and I pretended that we were about to attack. Easy. Bang! Goodbye, North Bend, Oregon. Back to Mars for tea.

## 12 JUNE 1958, NORTH BEND

Having a problem with my shoes that I got in Hong Kong. First it was the rain. It never dawned on me that you don't have brown or black leather – naturally, that is. The nice brown is not real and the dye isn't (wasn't?) much good. We had a run ashore for a meal. Not much to see, but we did it anyway. It was raining. We were sitting at the counter in this café place when Ainslie said, Sod me! Your sodding shoes are melting. The shoes were brown and white streaks. The dye was washing off. Then when we got back I was scrubbing off some of the dock mud and one of the heels came off in my hand. I suppose you can't get much for £4. Even in Hong Kong.

## 13 JUNE 1958, NORTH BEND

Fourth's a Mason. Second Mate says so. Said it's some secret society where they give each other jobs and wear aprons with their trousers rolled up, especially when they have these big dinners together. I gave him a look. But he seems to be serious enough. I said was he sure about the pinny? No doubt, he said. That sounds as if he's something else. Second Mate said probably that too, but take it from him the Fourth's a Mason.

We're going to Eureka. It's just down the coast in California. Imagine calling somewhere Eureka. Must have been the gold rush. I shall watch the gangway to see if the Fourth goes ashore in his pinny.

## 14 June 1958, Eureka

Ainslie's had a letter from his cousin. This cousin says he saw Veronica the other night with the bloke from Boots. He says he doesn't want to stir things but he thought Ainslie should know. Ainslie said to me that he thought it was only for old times' sake. I started to ask him how many old times' sake did she need? But I didn't. I just said that he was bound to be right. He said of course he was. I said of course he was. I'm learning to be subtle.

## 15 June 1958, Eureka

Most amazing thing this morning. I took my broken shoe to a mender in the main drag. They call it a heel-bar. You just give the shoe to the man and he fixes it while you wait. Dad's always done ours at home. He's got a proper cobbler's last in the shed and uses leather that's twice as thick as the mender's. It looks a bit heavy, but he makes a good job of it. Even does Mum's shoes. Anyway, there's a sort of café in this place, so I was sitting in one of the booths having chocolate pie and coffee with just one shoe on when someone leaned over the back and said, You English? He had a sort of American accent, but when I said I was, his voice changed and he sounded English. Where you from? I said a small place called Belvedere. He looked amazed. Where? Bedonwell Road, I said. Whereabouts? 244, I said. I live in Stream Way, he said. That's at the bottom of our garden. In fact, the council took a chunk of our garden to build the houses. He's working over here now, but his mum and dad still live there. I've never seen him in my life, but I remember his dog. Black and white Border collie who once ate Tippy, Auntie Heron's old tabby.

Once back at sea, out came the chipping hammers. So did the textbooks and the papers for the Board of Trade examinations he'd have to take. It wasn't all drudge. A lot was fun, and it was surprising how easy it was to feel exclusive about a few patterns in a clear Pacific sky.

## 21 June 1958, at sea, on passage from Eureka to Honolulu

I've learned all the main stars. I quite like knowing their names. Bellatrix. Sirius, Arcturus, Anilam. Soltar. Castor and Pollux. The Mate calls them cast-iron bollocks. Sirius is in the constellation of Orion and it's the brightest star in the firmament. He says it's the constipation of O'Brien and it's proper serious because he's got the tightest arse in the infirmary. He says that's the way to remember it. I said I thought I could remember it anyway. Don't think he was much impressed. It's pretty easy to offend.

It's very difficult on a ship. At home you can maybe never see anyone for days or just keep out of the way. On board, you see everyone all the time, or they see you. If you don't laugh when they do, then they make a decision about you. Mostly people are uncomplicated. But I think that once they've decided about you, that's it.

## 23 June 1958

Yesterday the stars. Today I now know about time. At least, I think I do. I thought that time was nothing more than that. Twenty-four hours a day. It is, but it isn't. Apparently there are two types of time. One is called solar time – that's what everyone knows about, or is supposed to – and the other is sidereal time – that's about stars.

This evening the Mate started talking about solar time. He says it's the ordinary twenty-four-hour thing which everyone understands. It comes from what the sun does every day. Or really what the sun appears to do, because it doesn't do what we think it does – like rise and set. According to the Mate, solar time is all about working out if the sun reaches a fixed point at the same time every day (which it doesn't) and, if not, where is it (late or early)? That I could see immediately, but then he said it was to do with what he calls the obliquity of the ecliptic and the eccentricity of the earth's orbit. He says the obliquity of the ecliptic is the angle between the ecliptic and the equinoctial. What, I said, is the ecliptic? There was a big pause.

'Don't they teach you anything at school these days, Chuck?'

I said I must have left before we got round to ecliptics. He didn't think that was very funny.

He said, 'Maybe they thought that you were too thick to take it on board.'

Maybe. But what is it? An ecliptic I mean. Dead simple, he said: it's the apparent path of the sun. Why apparent? Why not just say what it does? Another big sigh. Because, he said, we think it rises in the east and sets in the west, but it doesn't, because we're actually doing the going round. Like Galileo, I said. Sigh Number Three. I must remember it doesn't pay to be smart. Write this down, he said: The apparent motion of the sun is that it rises in the east and sets in the west once a day and each year completes one revolution of its orbit – that's the ecliptic.

I think that all this means is this: if I'm standing in the back garden in Belvedere at midday with the sun overhead and then I wait until it comes round again the next day, then the time for the sun to be overhead again will be different. As it's going from east to west, the gap between being overhead the first time and overhead the second time must be the only way in which we can measure what he calls real time. That means our sundial at home is always the right time – as long as you can see the rotten sun, of course.

He said, More or less. He says more or less quite often, which, I think, means I don't always get it right. So I drew a big circle and put a mark right at the top at noon, then pretended to wait for the sun to come round again, exactly twenty-four hours later. According to my drawing, the sun wouldn't be at the same point (that's the thing about ecliptics and the rest). Therefore (I think) the point between that mark and where the sun actually was twenty-four hours later is the only accurate measurement we have of time. So it doesn't matter where you stand on the earth, the distance between the two marks on the circle is how you can measure time. The Mate said that was more or less right and that the arc is called the Westerly Hour Angle.

I was feeling quite pleased with myself and then spoiled it.

I said it all sounded very convenient. Just because we say the sun comes up and goes down, why can't we think of it as going down first and coming up later. If we did that, we would reverse what we think is time. And why should we always think of time as going forwards? It might be going backwards. Maybe it doesn't exist. Maybe we're just making it up. He looked at me for about as long as it takes to smoke half a cigarette and then he said, Listen, Chuck, this is a navigation lesson, not a frigging seminar in metaphysics. Metaphysics? I must get a dictionary.

## 24 JUNE 1958

I'm now pretty certain the Mate was a bit grumpy with me yesterday. He's given me the most ginormous list of definitions to learn.

Right Ascension
Celestial Concave
First Point of Aries
Precession of the Equinoxes
Celestial Pole
Celestial Latitude and Longitude
Declination
Local Hour Angle
Sidereal Hour Angle
Greenwich Angle
Radius Vectors
Syzygy (which I think is just a fancy way of saying 'full moon')
Conjunctions
Zodiac Belt.

And he wants them by the morning. I said that with respect, sir, I didn't think he'd given me much time. He said, With respect,

Chuck, you're the great expert on frigging time: find some.

## 25 JUNE 1958

The bad news is that I didn't get the list right. The good news is that he didn't seem to mind too much. I suppose it proves him right – I'm not very bright. We're due into Honolulu in three days' time. We've made a good passage. Better than expected, and everyone's quite cheerful. That probably explains his mood.

## 29 JUNE 1958, HONOLULU

We're only here for bunkers. Can't even get ashore for a look. I was asking one of the oilmen about Waikiki. Great place, he said. White sand. Nice music. Beautiful girls. Not for you, boss, not for you. All this way and not even a go on a surfboard, never mind a pretty girl. Oh well, Australia can't be that bad.

## 4 JULY 1958

We're having a party. Actually, it's more than a party. It's a sort of ceremony. Crossing the line. Tomorrow we cross the equator. I reckon in the Pacific there's not much else to do but cross the equator. Everyone says it's just fun but takes it quite seriously. I'm not certain why.

We've spent all weekend getting ready for it. Even the Captain takes part. He's going to be King Neptune. Strange, really. I'm not sure why everyone's so chuffed. I mean, it's only crossing the equator. So what? I haven't asked anyone why it's so important and why we do all this stuff. It's not as if we're rounding the Horn in a force ten with just a storms'l and the cook's socks to steady us. There's an old book in the cupboard written by some admiral in 1860.* It's full of nautical things. But he doesn't say anything about crossing the line. I had a look at the chart last night. It's just a line.

On the chart maybe. Not in the sailors' lore. Crossing the line was important. The symbolism was enormous. True, nothing like Cape Horn in the old days of three-masters with torn royals and nine knots under bare poles. Then what could be? Nothing was like the Horn at its worst. And when the tales were told, it was always that – at its worst. Cape Horn in square-riggers was a powerful image. Hard men, often frightened. Wretched conditions. Magnificent seas. Superb seamanship. A combination of legends. A Cape Horner walked quietly to the bar. Nothing to prove. Others kept their bragging distance. So why was crossing the line so important? The sailor had now gone south (or north, depending on his home waters) of the equator, the line of zero latitude. In times past it was a frontier, the dividing line between the two hemispheres. North and south. South and north. If you sailed north from, say, Australia, then you were truly on your way to the Old World. Spices and mystery to starboard, enlightenment and origins to port. Whichever way you touched the tiller, picture books would come to life. When you sailed from Birkenhead or Bremerhaven, there were no picture books. Crossing the equator was entering the empty quarter of the oceans. True, five points to starboard, the sixth continent – but why go there unless it was to round the Horn? Steer east-sou'-east, and the dark continent and another cape.

*Admiral W. H. Smyth (1788–1865), *The Sailor's Word Book*, published posthumously in 1867.

Sail due south, and bleakness. The doldrums, then cold and horrific following southern seas. Then, so some had heard, ice. Most of all it meant distance. Only turning back would save you. Yet going south then east would mean the Orient. For centuries, prized cargo from rolls of finest silks to thin chests of scented teas. The clipper routes when men said they were bound for parts others only imagined. Before the coming of Suez, a ship had first to go south and cross the equator. So crossing the line, said a sailor, was properly deep sea. He'd got his knees properly brown. Could swagger a bit when he returned to Belvedere.

## 5 JULY 1958, THE EQUATOR

It's quite something, really. I was a bit nervous. Everyone dressed up. I had to make a big fish tail out of sacking and paint it silver with black scales. Why they picked me to be a mermaid I'm not sure. I even made a wig from old rope ends. Ainslie said I looked quite good. Keep an eye on the Second if I were you, he said. He'll quite fancy you. He does anyway. I've seen him looking at me quite a few times. I was scared at first. Not any more. He's harmless. Anyway, he's giving one of the greasers a seeing to.

We crossed the line at noon. Those of us who hadn't done it before got dragged before Neptune and then covered in all sorts of slosh. It was disgusting. Flour, ketchup and some slime from the galley. Then there was lots of chanting, and Neptune declared that we were proper sons of the sea and we had to sing. I sang the first verse of 'Phil the Fluter' because, apart from about six hymns, Nunc Dimittis and 'Heartbreak Hotel', it's the only thing I know more than one verse of. I thought I'd done quite well. The Fourth said it was really good but pity I didn't know the proper words. I thought I did. Maybe Masons and policemen sing different words.

So that's it. I suppose that means I'm real now. I can't be done again. Like being confirmed. Or maybe like being a soldier and going to war. The ones who don't go can't be proper soldiers, can they? The ones who stayed behind can't look the ones who went in the eye. I suppose it's the same. Next trip it'll be someone else. But it'll never be me again. I may be the youngest and most junior bloke on the ship, but I'm just as good as the rest. I've been south.

## 7 July 1958

Strange. I didn't think there was anything in this crossing the line thing, but there is. It's not the ceremony. That was just fun. It's as if everything I've always known has been untied. Until now it's been like I was on the end of a bit of string. We could sail down to Gib, or even the Red Sea, even India, and someone could tug me back. But once you go south of the equator, it really is another world. Space, I suppose. I told Ainslie and he said that was because there was less to bump into. That was funny, but in some way he's right. I got out an atlas. I never realised that most countries are at the top. I wonder why? I suppose if you were an Australian you could turn the map up the other way and say that you were at the top and everyone else was down under. It wouldn't work. No one would believe you. And if the Australians turned it upside down, then because of things like kings and paintings and religions and books and music, the important bit of the world would still be where all that was. I mean, our house was built before people went to Australia. Doesn't matter which way the world is up or down, it's what's up or down that matters. First time I've thought of it. I suppose everyone else has already done that.

What's different is the feeling. Almost as soon as we crossed the equator and started calling all the latitudes south, I knew it was different.

Sometimes when I've felt a bit homesick I've looked up and thought it can't be too bad because if Mum was looking up at the same time we'd be looking at the same sky. But that's not true now. I wrote to Mum and Dad this morning and told them that all the stars are upside down. I think that's right. The Mate says you see constellations at different angles. He says even the water goes down the plug the other way. He did explain, but I'm not sure what he meant. I'm not even sure that it's true, and the odd thing is that I won't know until we go north again, will I? This really is another world. The string's been cut.

## 11 JULY 1958

There are times when it would be nice to tell someone at home something I've learned that I'm pretty certain they don't know. I suppose that's called swanking. I'm learning about the zodiac. I thought the signs of the zodiac were just things that Mum talks about in the *Daily Express*. I know I'm Libra and so is Dad. Mum was born on 30 April, but I'm not sure which her sign is. What I didn't know is that it's all real. Well, sort of. The Mate says the zodiac is a belt of eight degrees on each side of the apparent path of the sun. In that belt are the moon and the planets. He says the belt is divided by twelve, which makes each section thirty degrees and each one is a sign of the zodiac.

I asked the Mate how it is we can tell the future from these thirty-degree sections. He said it was bullshit. Everyone's life is all about the weather. Spring people are optimists. Summer people are outgoing. Autumn people are not hot and they're not cold, so they're easy-going. Winter people huddle inside themselves. Then he said the world was simpler than people made out. People in cold places behave differently from people in warm places. They eat different foods, and one lot have jungles and the other lot have rocks, which means one's rich from what's in the ground and the other lot just have a load of trees. If you live in the cold, then it's easier to work, so you get rich and smart. If you live in the hot, then it's not. If you live in the hot you're black. If you live in the cold you're white. That, he said, is what makes the world tick, not Lord-friggin'-Luck in the *Daily Express*. I've written all this to Mum.

## 14 July 1958

We're in trouble. It's all about eggs. Sort of, anyway. We don't eat with the others. We have to eat in the smoke room, including breakfast. Every morning the steward says, What eggs you want? Every morning I say boiled, and every morning Ainslie says fried. Couldn't be easier. Not so. Every morning they get it wrong. If I get my eggs boiled its because the steward thought I said poached, or scrambled, or fried or even raw for all I know and got it wrong and brought me what I ordered. So on Monday Ainslie and I thought we'd rot them up. I ordered one boiled and one poached and Ainslie ordered one fried and one scrambled. They got it wrong so we sent them back. On Tuesday I ordered one scrambled and one boiled and got one poached and one scrambled and

Ainslie got two boiled. We tried it again on Wednesday, but the chief steward told the Mate. Next thing he's in. What the friggin' hell you playing at? He then told us to get out. Told the steward to issue us with a plate, knife and fork each and not to let us in. You want to act like a couple of little whores [he says 'whoo-ers'] then you'll be treated like a couple of little whoo-ers. So now we have to go to the pantry door and get whatever there is. If the officers haven't eaten all the scrambled, then it's scrambled for breakfast. I could get quite grumpy about cold fried eggs – sunny side up. When we get it, we have to eat it outside the pantry door on number three hatch. The Chinese crew think it's really funny. Ainslie is livid. Says one of the advantages of being white is that you don't have to beg. I said we should make placards and walk up and down outside the Captain's cabin and threaten to tell the Flying Angel padre. We won't. I wonder what would happen if we did?

## 19 July 1958

We're due in Sydney at 0800 tomorrow. It's about ten years ago since Uncle Eric came here with the Royal Navy in his aircraft carrier. He never came home. They transferred him to the Royal Australian Navy. I can't think why. He was always going on about the Navy being the best service in the world and Nelson being the finest sailor the world's ever known. Maybe he found out it wasn't true, like a lot of things his lot were told. Dad always says that we were supposed to have beaten old Hitler, but the Germans won the war because we're still hard up and they're all driving around in Mercedes-Benzes. I don't know about that, but Mum says Uncle Eric said the Navy was going down the pan and that's why he transferred to the RAN. Mum says he's already become an Australian and even sounds like one on the phone. Keeps saying things are beaut. She says the thing about Australians is that all their parents were convicts. The Mate says if it hadn't been for the Aussies and New Zealanders, we'd have been in trouble during the war. They always turn up, he says. Hope they haven't told Uncle Eric that. Dad reckons he's joined up because he wants to get as far away as possible in case we have a war with the Reds.

# 9

## MA GLEESON'S AND THE DRINK

These were the 1950s. Australia still dangled corks from its wide-brimmed hat. It saw life through half-closed eyes. Couth was something they had in Melbourne, and the train track from Sydney to Melbourne was lined with empty beer cans. Thousands, maybe millions of monuments to the nation's character. Sherry was kept in the refrigerator. The women wore floral frocks and the men rolled their mostly blue shirtsleeves above their biceps. They drove swaying Holdens and Fairlanes and shot kangaroos at midnight from trucks with searchlights. They drank themselves silly on ponies, midis, but usually schooners of cold Resches and Coopers between five and six in the evening, because after that the pubs were shut. They were surprisingly prudish. They said things like 'Strewth' and 'My flamin' oath' and called each other Mate. Men were Bruce. Women were Sheilas. Hooligans were larrikins. Even second-generation Australians, especially British, called migrants from Europe, 'refo bastards'. Greeks,

Poles and Balts were all refo bastards. 'Come down here, live on nothing but the smell of an oily rag and take all our jobs.' Mind you, they still paid them to fix their Holdens, Fairlanes and their plumbing. They treated 'abos' like dirt, but bought Namatachura's primitives just as Americans collected Grandma Moses. The Sydney Myer Music Bowl would be filled for the Czech Philharmonic as long as some flamin' fool hadn't booked them on Melbourne Cup Day. They would stand for the overture in case it might be the Czech national anthem. They were ruled by Robert Menzies, known to all as Pig Iron Bob, who was uncompromisingly pro-British except when it came to the ritual of beating the MCC touring side. They talked about the old country, and the youngsters promised they would go 'overseas', by which they meant Europe, starting with Britain. And if they said they'd call on you when they got to England, God help you, they would. Unlike their fathers, who solemnly stood before war memorials each Anzac Day, they went for pleasure. It was the land of the free and opportunity. Poms paid £10 to escape cold, austere Britain for a land of sunshine and opportunity, opportunity, that is, for anyone willing to work hard, which most British were not and never had been. It was, too, the land of the union boss, bosses who had followed not the anachronisms of the British system but the harsher and better-organised groups in America. Teamsters, not Transport Workers. A sense of don't-do-me-down-mate meant dustmen liked to be called garbologists. Dockers were waterside workers. Pity the employer who forgot this.

## 22 July 1958, Sydney

The wharfies are very powerful people. Every morning on the local radio, someone reads out what's called the Waterside

Workers' Call. It's just a load of numbers. More dockers listen to it than the football results because if you hear your number it means that you work that day. The unions run everything. I remember Pop talking about the shop stewards in his factory. The Aussies call them delegates. On board, the delegate's the most powerful man on the ship. He has a whistle, and if he blows it they all stop work. He'll blow it for the slightest thing if there's a dispute.

The delegate on our ship is called the High Court Judge. I asked one of the wharfies why they call him that. He pointed to the cargo. Him? Because he does fuck all and just sits around on all those cases.

This morning they stopped work again. The Second Mate was on at the time. What's the problem? It was the High Court Judge with his whistle. 'We ain't got no clouder and no pisser.

What's that mean, said the Second Mate.

Clouder has to watch the sky in case it rains and we have to stop work.

But it hasn't rained for ten weeks, said the Second Mate; there's a drought.

The High Court Judge gave him a big shrug. You never know. You never know, he said, and blew his whistle.

What's the other one that's missing?

The pisser? That's right mate. The bloke who goes below and relieves them when the pressure's too much for them.

All seems daft, but they stopped work for half the morning until they got a clouder and a pisser.

Last trip down here, or so the Second Mate says, some of the dockers broke open a crate that had whisky in it. The Second Mate caught them taking it and reported them. Next thing the delegate's blowing his whistle. They all went on strike for two days. The delegate says his wharfies were not stealing. The crate fell open and they were just looking after it and now they were insulted. The Second Mate had to apologise and was given a right bollocking for causing trouble and holding up the ship for two days which they say costs a lot of money. But even then the wharfies wouldn't go back to work until they'd got compensation. Anyway, now I'm for it.

The ship ahead of us has a strike on its hands. All loading's stopped. They've got a part cargo of lavatories. The wharfies demanded more money for unloading them. They said it was embarrassing to be seen carrying lavatory pans. I don't know who'd see them and even if they did, so what? They said they wouldn't work without embarrassment money. They've got it. But they're still not working because it has to be put to a vote. Presumably they're waiting for the clouder and pisser to vote. I was talking to a couple of the wharfies on our ship and I said I bet they wouldn't have asked for embarrassment money if it had been a cargo of whisky. Next thing this bloke's told the delegate and he's blowing his sodding whistle all over the place. He says I've insulted them. For a bunch of people who are supposed to be tough and couldn't care a toss about anyone, they really are touchy. The Mate had to apologise and explain that I was just joking and then had to apologise to the delegate with a bottle of whisky before he'd let them back to work. Then I was hauled in to the Mate's office and told I was a pillock and that my shore leave's stopped. That's not fair, and I told him. He said, Listen here, Chuck, fairness is what other people have, and the sooner you learn that the better.

## 24 July 1958, Sydney

These wharfies are very funny sometimes. Heard them calling Ainslie Lucky Legs. I asked one of them why.

'Well, he's got long thin legs, ain't he?

He has. He has. So what?

Well he's lucky they don't snap off and get stuck up his arse.

I told Ainslie. He didn't think it was funny at all and looked at me closely to see if I did. I told him it was outrageous. He hadn't heard me say 'outrageous' before and so wasn't sure if I was being nice or not.

## 27 July 1958, Wollongong

At last it's not me in trouble. Ainslie got arrested last night for stealing a car and driving it down the hill. He then collapsed. No stamina. That's the problem of being tall and thin. And drunk. This big red-faced rozzer about the size of a 122 bus arrived on board to see the Mate. I was on gangway-watch by the Mate's cabin. I could hear the Mate telling him that the lad had been working hard all day and was just relaxing. Strewth, said the policeman, hate to think what the bastard'll do when he puts his mind to it.

Maybe Ainslie will get six months on the chain gang. Mr Edgington [his history master] was brilliant about criminals being deported to Australia. The Fourth says Ainslie could get deported. I wonder what Veronica's mum would say? She probably thinks he's quite nice. It would certainly mess things up with Veronica if Ainslie went home clapped in irons. If they jailed him for life, perhaps I would go and explain things to Veronica. Never know what would happen. It's a strange thing to do, stealing a car, specially for Ainslie. He can't drive. Far as I know, he's never had a lesson in his life. Couldn't have done. He's been in the bottom bunk since he was old enough to drive. Likes a drink, though.

A sailor ashore went to the pub, the bar, the club, le café or wherever it was the locals served the stuff. In some places there were whole streets devoted to pouring booze down the throats of sailors and providing women, mostly women, when the drink had no more fun in it, or had done its work. In Hamburg Jack would head for the Reeperbahn, a blousy parade of bars, striptease joints and knocking-shops that was easily found off an otherwise respectable thoroughfare. In Hong Kong there was Lockhart Road and Hennessy Road. In Sydney there was Kings Cross, simply the Cross. The Gut in Valletta. Boogie Street in Bombay. South Pallafox Street in Pensacola. In the 1950s New Zealand was a great place, but not for a whole weekend. In Auckland the smart place to take a beer was at The Great Northern Hotel. But come six in the evening all the pubs and bars closed down. But sailors knew about Ma Gleeson's. To keep some of the law happy, Ma would sell a sailor a camp bed for the night – which he would never see – and then he could carry on drinking. The New Zealanders called this sort of place a sly grogger. It is a great tribute to New Zealand that Ma Gleeson's became the most famous sly grogger in the whole wide world. What was it about sailors and drink? They'd always done it. Then so had most people. Miners drank pints that looked like quarts. Haymakers drank scrumpy – the cloudier the better. Munitions workers were often so drunk that soldiers ran short of their own, but not German, bullets in the Great War trenches. Car workers drank mild and bitter and left nuts loose on doors that rattled. Vicars drank sherry. Surgeons, whisky. Dons, claret. Debs, champagne. The higher up the social scale, the paler the tipple, the more fragile the glass. Sailors drank anything. And, of course, they didn't go home. They didn't wait for Friday night. The pay-packet on the kitchen table. A note or two missing for the weekend. When a ship docked, the chief steward would draw the local currency. Jack was down the gangway. A month of Friday nights rolled into one. A run ashore meant a bar, usually within a brisk walk from the dock gate – and perhaps a stagger back. Bacardi in Havana. Bols in Rotterdam. Bex in Hamburg. Mao Tai in Tientsin. Suntory in Yokohama. Resch's by the schooner-load with two shakes from the busty barmaid at the Imperial in Sydney. Tiger in Singapore. Schnapps in Gdansk. Bud in Mobile. Sweet brandy in Gib. But never, never Chianti in Genoa. Sailors didn't drink wine in the 1950s. Stewards might. A deckhand never would. Booze was not an adventure. On the bridge at night, crossing a wintry North Atlantic, the sailor drank kai, a thick chocolate brew made with spoonfuls of thick condensed milk. A pint of iced water laced with Board of Trade lime juice as they sailed through a clammy Malacca Strait waiting for the dawn. Half-pints of tea in smoke-o, a precious fifteen-minute morning break. Maybe powdered coffee in a sturdy white cup after supper. On the rare occasions someone made a social call at another's cabin, then they'd maybe knock the top from a green-bottled Tuborg. A sailor's cabin was all he had. There was no other room. No kitchen to make a social coffee or tea. So a beer was sociable. And it was cheap. Duty-free. Two bottles of whisky and a few beers for a pound, although a wise skipper made sure they were rationed and even then allowed only among officers. A beer aboard ship was cheaper than a tram-ride to the nearest bar. Some might drink for oblivion. Most drank simply because they did. When a sailor had too much, there was no sympathy. No admiration. A skinful ashore only won the barman's medal. The bosun and the Mate gave no decorations, only orders. A return to the ship the worse for wear at sunrise mattered not too much as long as a deckhand was turned to with paintbrush, splicing fid or chipping hammer with the rest of them at eight. Sailors weren't special drinkers. They just had that reputation. Some, maybe many, worked hard at keeping it and, when there wasn't much else to do – no cinema, no television, no wife – they did that rather well.

## 29 JULY 1958, WOLLONGONG

Ainslie's not in prison. He's been fined. The Mate went down and paid it himself. Really nice. But the judge says he can't land in Australia for the next six months, or something like that.

The Second Mate said it would be a good idea if we had wine at special meals. What special meals, said the Mate. Special birthdays, or Christmas. I heard the Mate asking the Chief what he thought. The Chief, who knows a thing or two, said he thought the Second Mate was a bit suspect. Wine was OK on passenger ships – but it wasn't a real drink. He said he's seen some strange sights in London and New York with tramps lying in corners with wine bottles. Anyway, said the Chief, quite a lot of priests drink wine. I don't think the Mate saw the connection, but obviously the old Chief thinks there's something odd going on. Always does. The Mate said he'd mention it to the Captain. I bet he says no. The Captain doesn't like any drinking on board, especially at sea. The occasional beer's OK, but nothing else. He says it's too dangerous. Too easy to fall down a ladder or even over the side.

# 29 JULY 1958, WOLLONGONG

We went ashore last night with the Mate. It was really funny. The Mate paid Ainslie's fine but his shore leave's stopped. The Captain was walking up and down banging his fist on the bulkhead and giving the Mate a hard time as if it was all his fault.

'Don't let him near the gangway, mister,' he said. 'Tak' your eye off little booger and he'll be ashore like a flash o' pig-shit. A couple of swift bevvies and he'll have every bloody car in bloody Wollongong stacked, oop in't heap. See if I'm not reet.'

The Mate said he'd keep a personal eye on Ainslie. Don't think the Old Man knew what the Mate was up to. When it was dark, he came down and showed us how to make up a dummy, to make it look as if Ainslie was asleep. A joey, he called it. Then when he knew the Old Man was inside his cabin, we sneaked Ainslie down the gangway. Ainslie looked about nine feet tall and a bit daft in a mac in this climate. But we got ashore all right. I spent the whole evening waiting to bump into the red-faced copper. Why I should have been worried, I don't know. They weren't. The Mate knew a sly grogger and by midnight we were well away. It was about one in the morning before we got back to the wharf. Ainslie had to hide by the loading bay until we gave him the all clear. We got on board and there was the old Chief leaning on the rail. The Mate suggested he went into his cabin for a drink. But the Chief said he wanted some fresh air. We must have been standing there for about an hour waiting for the Chief to go to bed, but he just kept sucking on his pipe and talking about the good old days. Then we heard this noise. It was Ainslie peeing against the loading bay wall. Ainslie is a noisy pee-er at the best of times. But at one in the morning after six pints of beer against a corrugated iron shed, the whole of Australia could hear him. The Chief looked down but he couldn't see anything. Dirty bastard down there, he said. Bloody swagman or whatever they call them. Then he went to bed. Ainslie was raging by the time we got him back on board. He pushed into the cabin and the next thing gives this mighty shout. There's some bastard in my bunk, he yells. With that he leaps at his bunk and starts beating shit out of the Mate's joey.

## 30 July 1958, Wollongong

Ainslie says that a couple of trips ago they had a Mate who was drunk a lot of the time, even on watch. What happened? He said the Captain had him sent home for medical reasons. I said I thought it was sad. Ainslie just laughed and said I knew nothing. He said the last time he heard of him, the Mate still had his ticket and was Captain of some old London Greek with a dago crew and the whole sodding ship was drunk and probably going round and round in a big circle in the middle of the Atlantic.

When the orders came through to set a course for Nauru, it meant The Tramp was on the dreaded phosphate run. Dreaded because it was filthy and mostly boring. Nauru is a coral island in the Pacific, about half a degree south of the equator and 160-something degrees east. Pretty much on her own in the world. If you sailed dead north from her, you'd probably not hit anything until you saw the most eastern end of Russia – in those days, the Union of Soviet Socialist Republics. South, then you'd have a reasonably straight run along a line of longitude to the Antarctic. Not many people go to Nauru. It's an oval blob of coral with a lagoon, a stretch of beach and a central plateau of phosphate – or at least it had when The Tramp arrived. Nauru was 'discovered' by a Captain Fearn in 1798, the year Nelson was beating up Napoleon's fleet at the Nile, or close by. Ninety years later, the Germans took it: Nauru, that is. In 1914 the Australians took it from the Germans. Its strategic value was nil, Its commercial value high. The Pacific Phosphate Company was digging out the stuff even in the nineteenth century, and after the Great War, in 1919, the British, Australians and New Zealanders bought the mining rights for £3.5 million. A lot of money in those days. But then phosphate was worth a lot of money. Still is. The locals were looked after and everyone made fortunes. In 1967 the British Phosphate Corporation handed over the mining to the Nauruans. Why not? The phosphate was running out. The lad didn't know much of this. Dig it out. Ship it. Make a profit. That was about it in 1958.

## 10 August 1958, near Nauru

We're due into Nauru in a couple of days. It's on the other side of the world from home. Not exactly, but more or less. If I could drill a hole through the earth, then I could see our house. More or less. Really on the other side of the world. No connection at all. Once you've come south, you're in a different world, and now I'm right opposite anything I've always known. I looked at the atlas again. At home, you move your finger a bit and you're in France or Germany or Ireland. Here, you're still in the Pacific. No shapes. No people speaking. No people at all. Throw a bit of wood in the water in Hastings and it'll be in France maybe by the morning. Throw something over the side here and it'll be here for ever. I feel that. It's the South Pacific, and it's because there's nothing next to you but more ocean. The Mate says it's what he calls 'a sense of distance'. I think it's a sense of time. I can't imagine how long it would take to see anything again, and so I don't know that there's anything to see. In the north, you can cross the International Date Line and it doesn't mean so much. Because it's mostly land, I felt that although I was further away from home there was only distance between me and everyone I know. When you're in the north, you know if you just keep going, then you could eventually walk back the way you've come. There's nothing impossible between you and what you've left. Rivers and mountains and things, but you know what they are and where they are. It's like looking at hills, you know there has to be something over the other side and that when you get to the top, then you'll see what it is. Maybe even recognise it. I think I know what I mean. In China you can get a train home. Change at Moscow and the Hook for Liverpool Street. But here in the Pacific it's different. The closer you are to the water, the less distance there is and therefore there's no future. So you're just here. It's a sort of cloud kingdom without ways out. I know how to set a course for Panama, or the Horn or Suez and the rest comes. That's the navigation and the fact. But there's something else which you can't work out in columns of figures and multiply with cosines to get the answer where you are and how far you are from where you want to be. When there's no land, just ocean, and when you're sailing across the fattest part of the earth, then for a moment there's a strange feeling that the globe itself is between you and home. Maybe it's something to do with being on the equator. I'm on the fastest bit of a huge roundabout and I can imagine spinning off. Scary in a way. I'm not going to read what I've just written because I know it sounds daft. But it's what I feel.

## 11 August 1958, Nauru

Got into Nauru this morning. There's no proper harbour, just a titchy thing for small boats. We're moored fore and aft to big black wooden piles. These are supposed to be the deepest moorings in the world. This is a proper coral island straight out of a story book. Hardly any size at all. You could go straight by if you got your navigation a little bit wrong. There's a sandy beach, but not much of it. And it's mighty deep here. I looked at the chart. A bit out from the mooring there's nothing at all. The sea goes straight down for ever. It's as if we're sitting on a mountain-top, miles high. I suppose we are. Take the water away and you're left with mountains and valleys like the rest of the world. The Fourth says that in the Atlantic there are mountains bigger than Everest. That's five miles high, and there's still miles of water over them. The Fourth says that two-thirds of the world is covered with water. If someone had said that in class, I'd have thought about it, I suppose. When you're actually looking at an empty ocean and you know that there are enormous kingdoms of Everests and Grand Canyons down below, then you really understand how amazing the world is. It's not a big, smooth orange at all, is it? It's a wonder it goes round without mountains and things breaking off.

Before we got in, we had to put cloth in all the ports then screw the scuttles down really tight, then screw down the dead-lights [round metal shutters] over them. All the cabin and engine room vents have to be blocked off. It's the phosphate. It gets everywhere. It's like creamy-brown talcum powder. And it's not in bags. We'd got the tarps and hatch covers off by the time we came alongside. Soon as we'd tied up, enormous gantries were swung over with wonky chutes on the end. They just pour the phosphate into the holds. Miles of overhead buckets, then into hoppers, then down these chutes. It's everywhere. Eyes, nose, ears. Everywhere. So much for the romantic South Sea Islands. The stuff loads so quickly that you can almost see the ship drop down to her marks. There's a bloke called Ross who's in charge of it all. He's out of a picture book. Quite old – about fifty, I suppose. Big with a perfectly round beer belly and a nose like a massive red pumice stone. Wears khaki baggy shorts and a boundary rider's hat. That's what he used to do, he says. Boundary rider. Ride for miles fixing fences. Living rough. Campfires. Clipping on to telegraph wires to make contact. Just like 'Waltzing Matilda', I said. Too right, mate, too right. I thought he was taking the mick, but he's real enough.

# 10

## PASSAGE TO INDIA

Having loaded the phosphate, the next task was to get rid of it. Some ships simply plodded up and down. Up to Nauru. Down to Australia and New Zealand. Up to Nauru. Down to wherever. Lucrative for the shipowner, which is why they were there. More than a job. It was, it had to be, a way of life. A clerk, a toolmaker, a drummer did what clerks and toolmakers and drummers do and then went home and got on with their other lives. Being at work was, in those days, an interlude in their 'real' lives. Being at home was an interlude in a seaman's 'real' life.

So where they sailed, how often they sailed there and what happened while they were doing it was instinctively important to each of them – and in differing ways. Some liked the short haul between, say, Nauru and Ma Gleeson's. Others liked to keep moving. Liked tramping. Maybe in some of them, maybe in many of them, a sense of the hobo, the bum. The Tramp now sailed north. Into trouble.

When they'd fixed the cargo, it should have been eight days discharge' in Colombo, in what was then Ceylon. Then up the east coast to Madras and down to Cuddalore. Nice trip. Not so. When The Tramp arrived off Ceylon, the port was closed. It was like planning a trip to the Grand Canyon only to find it shut for Thanksgiving or something. It seemed impossible. But then, as the Mate said, embuggerances always do. The cargo couldn't go elsewhere. Both anchors were run out. It would be a long wait.

## 4 SEPTEMBER 1958, COLOMBO

Anchored off Colombo shortly after eight this morning. The dockies are on strike. Want bigger rice bowls or something. So here we stay. This morning the Mate said we'll get mail OK. They'll bring it out in a boat. He was right. A boat came alongside at noon. But the nig-nogs wouldn't hand it over until we sent down a carton of cigarettes. The steward thought he was clever and lowered some wartime fags called Convoy. The bumboatmen sent them back. Only American Lucky Strikes get the mail. Mate said we're going to be here for a long time. I said something about being hot and couldn't we go for a swim? Ainslie said if I want to be eaten by sharks, then that was fine by him, he could do with the extra locker space.

Part of the Mate's job was to keep the ship happy. Lying at anchor off Colombo among a flotilla of fifty or so other ships, in a continuous swell, was all right at first. The routine took care of itself. Always someone on the bridge. Checking the ship's position against shore bearings. Making sure she wasn't dragging anchors. Keeping an eye on other ships, day and night, to make sure they were secure. On deck, the hands carried on as normal. Hatch covers and corner boards were turned back to air the cargo. Vents were turned to fetch the wind for the thousands of tons of cargo below. Chipping and scraping and painting. Rust runs scraped and wired-brushed away from superstructure and winches. Red lead or yellow chromate paint on the bared patches. White paint on top of that until she dazzled in the Indian Ocean sunlight. Then came the decks. Chipped and scraped down to the metal. Then more red or yellow sloshed on with tough old bristles that wouldn't wear away in a morning against the steel plating. Right into the corners of the tightest scuppers, where the deck meets the ship's side and rails. After that, more sloshing. Slosh, slosh, slosh. Making up rhythms and lyrics. Slosh go the shears boys. This time red deck paint. On the bridge and boat decks, the same again, only this time the casab doled out the green deck paint. Red, yellow, white and green monotony. Had to be done otherwise she'd sink. For an old tramp, she was plenty smart.

The Third Mate was in charge of the lifeboats. It was a good time to service them. The canvas covers off and scrubbed then patched. The emergency stores checked. Number three boat, the only one with an engine, turned over in a splutter of black fumes and a cussing Third Engineer. Had to be done. In a crisis, it was number three boat that would tow the others off. And if she didn't get away? Ask, and the answer was a shrug. The heavy black derrick blocks were stripped and greased. The topmast painted black. The boat deck awnings respliced. The cabins painted out for cockroaches. The black edging tiles in the heads boiled oiled until they shone for the Master's Sunday forenoon inspection – he took care not to slip on the crew's handiwork. It wasn't that he was likely to say much. It was all about getting the crew to keep her shipshape to stop him having to. Yet there came the time when the Mate needed diversions to keep everyone reasonably happy.

We're going to build a swimming pool. I was up in the chartroom and heard the Mate talking to the Old Man. He said he thought we needed a project. People could start to get ratty, he said. We could be stuck out here for another couple of months. It was getting even hotter, so a swimming pool seemed logical. I went down to the cabin and told Ainslie. He said there was nowhere to put a swimming pool and, anyway, where would we get all the tiles and stuff to make one? He said what did I think this was, a friggin' cruise liner or something? He said just like my navigation I'd got it wrong, as usual. About half an hour later, just before smoke-o, I was painting the rail outside the Mate's cabin when I heard Ainslie in there suggesting to the Mate that wouldn't it be a brilliant idea to make a swimming pool? Just for morale, he said. The thing I like about Ainslie is that you know what's coming.

Sailors are resourceful fellows. At sea, a merchant ship has to make do with what she has on board. A destroyer can call up a store-ship, and perhaps within hours the fleet auxiliary will be standing off. A line will be fired over to the warship, ropes, pulleys and slings connected, and a well-rehearsed Replenishment At Sea routine will take place. Everything from mailbags to missiles will swing from mother to lethal child within an hour, and all without stopping. Indeed, it's easier to do it all steaming in parallel lines to each other. Nothing like this in merchantmen. The very history of a sailor and his vessel was simple and unchanged for centuries. The sailing master put to sea in the best vessel he could afford for his needs. He worked out the length of voyage and what might happen during that trip. He then had another look into his purse (hence 'purser' in merchant ships, 'pusser' in warships) to see what stores he could afford to take. There was no point in stowing food that would rot by the seventh day of a ninety-day voyage unless it was to be eaten by the seventh day. But what about things that might go wrong? How did the sailor predict what he would need on board? In sailing days, spare canvas, strong steel sewing needles to go through the toughest duck. Hemp twine and beeswax to make it easier to sew and less likely to chafe and break. Drums of deck paint. Grease for the derrick wires. Knives and fids for the deckhands. Spanners and hammers for the engine room. Reels of rope, some just needle-thick for whipping, splicing and running up signals, some sturdy and unforgiving as a flagpole. In an emergency, it was all make do. A sailor was rarely surprised by an emergency. For centuries sailors had known full well that they lived in the best of all possible worlds. It was a world of making the best of all that was possibly at hand. The craft of sailing is uncomplicated. Before engines, there were more things to go wrong. Ships had masts, spars, yards and royals, spankers and clews, luffs and blocks, caulking and strakes. When a stem head cracked, a topmast split, a bilge sprang, a halyard shredded, then whatever was at hand was used to fix, patch and hope. The instinct had survived into steam. Jury-rigging was second nature. If something broke and couldn't be repaired properly, then it was jury-rigged, patched up. A broken steering gear was fixed so that the vessel could continue on her way, albeit tentatively under the jury-rig. Why jury? 'Ajurie' is an Old French word. It means help, or aid. In the sixteenth century, sailors thought it good enough for them. So tell a sailor that number three 'tween deck hatch coaming has been bent and that the after top block is seized on number four davit and that the galley fiddly is jammed and the second cook is suffocating and he'll say something along the lines of, 'Aye, aye, sir', or maybe 'OK, boss', and think of something to fix them all. But a swimming pool in an old tramp ship lying at anchor off Colombo?

## 16 September 1958, at anchor still

The Great Swimming Pool is to be built. I was going to tell Ainslie I told you so, but he's in a bad mood. I think he's had another letter from Veronica. I know her envelopes. She writes in purple ink so the whole ship knows when he's had a letter. The last time she wrote he said she wanted to know how long it would be before he was home. I said that it was nice to be missed. The Third Mate said she probably just wants to know how long she's got to get whoever it is who's giving her a seeing-to out the back door before Ainslie comes through the front. Seems he knows her. I'm quite glad I don't have anyone to write to. It all seems disappointing. Anyway, we won't have much time to think about things like that for the next two days. The Mate says the pool's got to be built by Saturday and that it's going to be opened officially by the Captain. I asked if he was going to jump in it or something. The Mate said he thought he'd just say a few words. I said I still thought it would be really nice if he jumped in. Ainslie said I was a mouthy little sod and no one cared a toss what I thought and to nip for'd sharpish and tell the chippie that the Mate wanted him. Chong Ah Ping is really going to build the thing. We're just his navvies. That was shortly after breakfast this morning. By smoke-o at ten-thirty the whole thing was off. No one had told the Chief.

The Chief, the Chief Engineer, would sometimes see himself on a par with the Captain of a ship. The Captain wore four gold rings on his sleeves. So did the Chief. To tell the difference, the Chief had purple between his rings. That told everyone he was an engineer, just as the white rings between the two gold bands on the chief steward's sleeve told everyone what he did. Most important to the deck officers, this made clear that engineers weren't Mates. Engineers and Mates. Oil and water. Not always a good mixture. Yet the engineer had usually done a long shoreside apprenticeship, whereas the Mates were examined for the first of their 'tickets' – their Certificates of Competency – within at the very most four years of going to sea. The differences were obvious to anyone who had just a passing under-standing of society. An engineer was trade. A deck officer was profession – or so they liked to think. These were the 1950s when, in Britain at least, engineering was still seen as a second-grade job. The Tramp now carried the lad from door to door of the crumbling British colonial system. The Empire had been built by traders and engineers. The success of Victorian Britain had been built by engineers. Men had made fortunes from gears, pistons and machined circumferences true to the finest vernier scale. And when they had their fortunes, did they stand proud with their sons and send them to the shop floors to build on those foundations? Not a bit of it. They sent their sons to the public schools and into the professions. Engineers wanted 'better' for their offspring. It was trade. Had to be. You got dirty doing it. Lathes, spanners and overalls. Even in his best clothes at a ship's party, you could always tell an engineer. He'd instinctively wipe his hand on his trousers before shaking hands. That's what they said, anyway. The engineer would point out that the ship would never go if it weren't for him. The Mate would say that the ship would never know *where* to go if it weren't for him. Then he would add, And an engineer could never be Captain. But there was still a pecking order. Whatever they thought on deck of engineers as a breed, there was always a professional respect for the Chief. He wore four rings. He was the only person other than the Captain who had a day cabin as well as a night cabin – ashore they called it a bedroom. What was more, the Chief had his own bathroom. Even the Mate himself had to go all the way from his port-side cabin, which doubled as his office, to the starboard side to use the communal bathroom and lavatory. The Chief was somebody, all right. With a bit of thought, the Mate might have decided that the best place to put the timber and canvas Heath Robinson affair that he was calling a swimming pool was anywhere but right outside the Chief's main-deck portholes.

## 17 September 1958

The Chief's very upset. Has been since yesterday morning. It started with a discussion between the Mate and the Second Mate about where we should build the swimming pool. It's a dead simple idea. We make a box out of spare hatch boards. They're about eight or ten feet long and about two and a bit inches thick. The box will be about twelve feet long and about eight feet high. Then we sew an old tarpaulin into a bag shape the same size, put it in the box, fill it up with sea water and that's it. As a special privilege, Ainslie and I are to be allowed to scrub the tarpaulin clean. That seems simple except, as the Second Mate said, the problem is where to put the thing. It's very big. The hatch boards weigh a ton, and once it's filled with water the whole thing will be really heavy. And it takes up a lot of room. The Mate wondered about the boat deck, but the Second Mate said it was too heavy and, anyway, it needs to be close to a hydrant and scupper to keep filling and emptying. The place with most space is abaft the main accommodation on the afterdeck by number four hatch.

But the Mate said we might keep it up so that we could use it when we put to sea again, so it would be in the way of unloading and loading cargo. Also, if it's on the afterdeck, then all the Mates would have to walk miles to get to it. And there's something else: the pool is for officers only. Ainslie said that if it's on the afterdeck then the Chinese would be nipping in and out at night. I said, What's wrong with that? He said, they'll piss in it. Does that mean they don't like us? No, he said, it's just the sort of thing Chinese do. They piss in everything. That leaves only two places it could go. Either in front of our cabin on the starboard side, where it would be out of the way when we start cargo, or in the same position on the port side. The problem with our side is that the only working door to the galley is there, and the stewards would have trouble squeezing by when they fetched food for the officers' saloon. So that leaves the port side – which is right in front of the Chief's cabin.

About nine o'clock this morning we started to lug the hatch boards down over to the port side and the chippie was sawing up the first ones when there's this: Hoi! Hoi! What's going on? The chief's got his funny little bald head sticking out of his port and his pipe's wagging up and down.

It's OK, Chief, we're just building a swimming pool, says Ainslie.

Chief went purple. A what? he asked.

A swimming pool, Chief, says Ainslie again, then I thought a bit unnecessarily he added: We're going to swim in it.

The Chief's pipe went faster and started to send out streams of blue smoke. Oh no. Not in front of my cabin, you're not, he said.

It came out as a bit of a snarl, otherwise I suppose he'd have dropped his pipe. He's a sort of Scottish Popeye. In went his head and the next thing he's out on deck in his baggy shorts and flip-flops, his little hairy legs going nineteen to the dozen heading for the Captain's ladder. The Mate was just coming out, but the Chief went straight by muttering something about 'bloody little toerags' and 'I'm not having this' and disappeared up the ladder and into the Captain's flat. The Mate looked a bit surprised, so Ainslie told him what had happened. The Mate started scratching his arms as he always does when there's trouble and said it was best to go for a smoke-o.

Apart from the Mate and the radio officer, the Chief Engineer would have been the only one on board with direct access to the Captain. Just as the skipper kept himself apart from his deck officers, so the Chief held his engineers at arm's length even though they lived along the same alleyway. In the evenings the Chief might call on the Captain for a tipple and a chat, never staying long. On other evenings the Captain would visit the Chief, he, too, keeping faith with their only sea-going social event. In private, they were on first-name terms. Never in public. The Chief would use his right of access sparingly. It had to be important. Close to a crisis. The decision by the Mate to build a socking great tarred hatch board and tarpaulin contraption (the Chief never would bring himself to call it a swimming pool) right outside the Chief's cabin was a crisis. The crisis was caused, of course, not by the pool but by the flux of oil and water. The Mate had not even thought to consider the feelings of an engineer, not even the Chief Engineer. Engineers did not have feelings, only spanners.

## LATER

The Old Man sent down for the Mate and closed the outer door.

Ainslie says that's a bad sign. After about half an hour he reckoned it was all over. We were on our second tea and wondering if we had to lug all the hatch boards back to the poop deck. It's really hot today. Ninety-six degrees, according to the bridge thermometer and that's in the shade. I said, Let's do it this evening when it's cooler. Ainslie was sort of working to that idea, but because I'd said it he said we'd do it now. That was about noon. Great stuff, Ainslie. But we didn't have to because just then they came on to the Old Man's deck. The Mate was still scratching his arms. The Old Man was nodding. The Chief's pipe was upside down. I wondered if the baccy was going to fall out over his feet. He kept shaking his head and the upside-down pipe was a bit like those pictures of Roman emperors saying they think the gladiators and lions are a load of rubbish. Ainslie said it was best to keep out of the way, so we went off for another tea. The duty steward said we couldn't have any because the hot-water geyser wasn't working and he was fed up with all the rowing over a crazy pool. He's really pissed off because him and the rest of the Chinese know they'll not be allowed in. Then the Third Mate came in the pantry and told us to get out in our working gear. Said if we behaved like navvies we'd be treated like them and said that he wanted the lifeboat davit wires greased. I said we'd done that last week, and he said if I answered back again he'd have my shore leave stopped. I was about to say that seeing as we're anchored two miles off the sodding coast, fat lot of good that would do. Then the bosun turned up and said he'd got two deckhands sick and what was the Third Mate going to do about it? The Third Mate said he would kick their arses because they were probably just lazy bastards. The bosun said, This fashion speak no good. I could see the Third Mate had that look in his eye which means that when he gives the sailors a jab, he'll get through to the braces with the rotten needle. Just then the chief steward turned up muttering that his pantry wasn't the ship's office and the bum-boats were now demanding two cartons of cigarettes. Ainslie said drop a cargo hook on the black bastards and see how many Lucky Strikes the sharks would give them. It's one of those days. When people get really grumpy, the whole ship gets grumpy. No wonder the Mate wants a swimming pool. At least it will give the Third Mate something to think about instead of sodding lifeboat wires and stopping my shore leave. When we came out of the pantry, there was the Chief, the Mate and the Old Man over on the port side. The Chief's got a stick of yellow chalk and he's bent double like a stunted rhinoceros drawing lines athwartships. And that was it. Ah Kan, the cocky little quartermaster who's always got his vents on the wind, said the Mate had to apologise and explain. The Old Man then was really clever. According to Ah Kan, he says to the Chief, Well, Chief, we need your advice. This is all to do with morals. Where do you think we should put it?

I think Ah Kan means morale, but in a funny sort of way he's probably right even if the Old Man didn't say it like that. Anyway, that's why the Chief was drawing lines. We now have to build the swimming pool in his yellow chalk square. Seems to me that it's only three feet from where we were supposed to put it anyway. He reckons he's going to keep watch to make sure we don't cross the lines. Ainslie says the Chief's full of shit and it goes to show that he's got nothing else to do. Chippie says the Captain's a very wise man. Ainslie just smirked, but I wouldn't mind betting that he'll take the first chance of telling the Old Man something similar. Strange. I don't think Ainslie's a greasy sod like the Fourth says he is. I think it's just a game. Then, as the Fourth said tonight, the whole rotten day has been a game of something. You wouldn't think we'd have all this silly stuff without going anywhere. Although I suppose that's it. Just lying here at anchor is not what we're at sea for.

The pool became a monument at which proper respect for position and pecking order was observed. When the Captain visited it, then no one else did. Just as the Captain kept to himself in his cabin and his part of the bridge, so he kept his isolation in the pool. Indeed, no one watched, although a few saw. He would leave his cabin at eight in the evening and step smartly down the ladder to the main deck. A strange sight. Smart blue, shiny swimming trunks with an outlandish towelling yellow robe with blue ducks on it. No one remembered having before seen it (and they would have, surely?) and none saw it again. Even his steward claimed he had never noticed it in his locker (and he would have, surely?). The robe was folded over the top rung of the boarding ladder and the Captain slipped without fuss (he had never been known to) into the seawater pool. The Sparks, the radio operator who lived up on the bridge deck, claimed to have watched him from his cabin port. He neither swam nor dived, but floated. He floated with barely a flicker of his outstretched arms, with long pink big toes pointing skywards like two lost bobbins. He stayed that way for precisely twelve minutes, when, either from boredom or discipline (he must have been counting for he wore no watch), he would flap his hands to take him back to the ladder, stand with a shudder rather than a full body-shake at the edge of the pool, don the robe and smartly yet without hurry return to his quarters. If he met anyone on his way, there'd be no acknowledgement and none was sought. It was as if he had never been there. Apart from that quarter-hour in the evening, the pool was a free-for-all. All officers, that is. The Chinese pee a lot.

## 29 October 1958, Colombo

At last. Weighed anchor at eight this morning. Fifty-six days out here. Thought we were going to be here for ever. There's been close on a hundred ships anchored off.

## 30 October 1958, Colombo

Went to the office by the Port Commissioners to drop in the cargo permits. It's the place where the locals get their driving licences. They've got two windows. One says MEN and the other says WOMEN & INCURABLES. That's telling them.

As ever in port, there was a Flying Angel, a sympathetic haven for a deck apprentice with no money but a hope to see more than the dock gates and the main drag. Ceylon's padre wasn't ordained into the Church, only the way of life. Neat. Well pressed. Galle Face Cheltenham. Always had a round tin of fifty Three Roses cigarettes. He wasn't a heavy smoker. Just carried the tin. A nice man who had gone into colonial service straight from the Second German War, as he called the bloody 1939–1945 conflict. A man with a Plumb Warner view of the world; as if some international code had been written into laws drawn and laid down by the MCC. No great intellect. Great sense of honour and a gentle understanding of the middle-class values of the seaman. The officers with five Ordinary Level General Certificates of Education. The deckhands cleanly reliable and patient unless they were a Liverpool or Glasgow 'crowd', when the rules of polite conduct were swept aside shortly after the tenth bottle of Tiger. The Flying Angel man in Ceylon tended towards the Mates and engineers.

The Flying Angel padre reckons that these people are nicest of the Indian types. Of course, he said, most of them are heathens. I said, What does that mean? Buddhists, he said. But, he said, there's more than a million Christians. His face brightened up at that. I'm not sure why. He may be the sort of padre, but he lives like a bigwig. He's got a couple of houseboys who'll do anything for him. They do all his dhobi, cook his breakfast, the lot. I said I thought all that had changed. He reckons it's just the same. The houseboys reckon they've got a cushy number and they get a lot of status because he's quite important. He says it's just like the Raj and like it used to be when he was a kid in England. The servants are rated by the importance of their bosses. He says that one day the world will realise that being ruled by the British was the best thing that ever happened to them. Says he was in East Africa as a district officer. He calls it 'rather pleasant' and says that everyone knew their places and that he always did his best for the natives. The way he lives, I reckon they're doing their best for him. I was getting on fine with him, but he's a bit strange. We went out to the Galle Face Club with him for a swim. They got more servants than you can shake a stick at. I told the padre that my dad would think this funny – me getting waited on like this. Why should he, he said. Because he was a fisherman, then a chauffeur, then on the buses. He got a bit cool after that.

What did a lad do with his past when he went to sea? He probably didn't have much of one. He wasn't very old, and his working-class background assumed that he had no history.

In the 1950s a family of inshore trawlermen, fitters and turners, bombardiers and bus inspectors, and not a few on first-name terms with the bailiffs, was not the smart pedigree it became just a decade later. By the late 1960s it was fashionable to have mean beginnings and even invent them. In the 1950s plenty wanted to go up, few pretended to want to go down. Not yet. In previous decades, young lads may have been unhappy with their lot, but they didn't abandon it in order to get on. In the 1950s a social phenomenon of expectancy rather than simple hope wafted over the British Isles. The dissatisfaction that had influenced his parents' generation in the 1930s and tossed out the Tories in 1945 now settled on the lad's thoughts. Parents disillusioned. They hadn't even won the war. Any war. The Second World War had come and gone and there were still bomb sites with rickety cars for sale and buddleia sprouting from smashed walls and leaning stacks. The sense that there had to be something better peppered the chat at the kitchen table. But what did he want? What did he want people to think he wanted? How best to get it? Of course, he didn't know the answers to any of these questions. Indeed, it was unlikely that he even knew the questions. Getting away to sea was something inside him. The coasterman going deep-sea. Never heard of Conrad. He'd read a dry-leaved copy of Slocum. Maybe that had done it, or started it. But the real magnet had been the big funnels and the beauty of the cargo ships that navigated the Thames from estuary to Royal Docks. Yet when he eventually trod those hard decks, it was neither as a hand nor a steward, where no one had to be anyone. He was told that he was officer material. Keep your nose clean, lad, you could make it one day. Get yourself some confidence, the Third Engineer had told him. They like people with background, especially in passenger ships. A harsh transition for a lad from a small bedroom and a crossbar on his dad's bike down the hill after work.

He could invent a past. He could invent a family. Quiet remarks that might make the unsuspecting think there was an aristocrat hidden somewhere. Maybe someone on his maternal grandmother's side. Most lads of his age and background probably never knew their grand-mothers' maiden names anyway. And there really had been talk about a knight in the Civil War – a Royalist, of course. Even a minor canon. Or he could travel lightly with the little baggage he understood. There had to be something with which he might protect himself. But from what? Looking foolish. Foolishness, the social acne of 1950s youth. A youth made to know their place from toddler times. Their generation would be the one to abandon authority over their children. For now, the lad had what his age dealt him. He was on his own in a grown-up world. Others of his age went off to work, a very, very few to college, some to barracks. There they were all of a likeness and all of the same age. They still had time to grow. But this lad was just halfway through his teens. Adults still meant authority. Yet here he was thrown in and expected to be an adult. His imagination and his instincts might get him through.

### 3 NOVEMBER 1958, COLOMBO

Had a letter from Mum. She says everyone's well and that she hopes I am. I wonder why? You would think that with all those aunts, cousins and friends, at least one person would be ill. And why does she hope I'm well? Does she know something? Is there something she hasn't told me? Do people suddenly get something bad when they get to be seventeen or eighteen? I suppose it's something to say when there's nothing to say. It's like who you are. In this ship I know everyone, but I don't know who anyone is. No one really talks about their private lives. I suppose because they have two: this one at sea and the one they leave at home. If

we all started talking about them we'd mix them up. The Second
Mate asked me what Dad did for a living. When I told him, he
looked surprised. I thought he'd be more than that, he said. Then
he looked embarrassed and said he was sorry, he didn't mean it to
sound like that. I know what he means. Perhaps it's me. Perhaps
it's because I went to Rosie Bru's [Rose Bruford – drama school]
on Saturdays and listened to the BBC. Maybe I don't sound as if
I come from where I do. Part of me doesn't want to. The biggest
part of me does, but I'm beginning to see that people always want
more from you than you've got. That's sad, and it's really difficult
if you don't know what you've got.

## 4 NOVEMBER 1958, COLOMBO

We're going up to Madras then some place called Cuddalore. I
looked in my atlas and it's not there. It'll be on the chart, I
suppose. It's there right enough, matey, said the Sparks. Strange
bloke, the Sparks. Calls everyone matey, except the Captain, of
course. Keeps writing to the mayor or someone in Papeete, Tahiti.
Tells this bloke that he's planning to sail there in a yacht or
something. What yacht, I asked him. Don't you worry about me,
matey, I know what yacht it is. I asked him when he plans to go.
He just winked. I wish people wouldn't wink. I never know if it's
because they think you're in the secret or they know you're not.
Auntie Eva was always winking. But she'd got something wrong
with her, although Uncle Frank always reckoned it took the
parson a long time before he realised he wasn't in there with a
chance. Sparks does it deliberately. Winks. Then taps the side of
his nose. He's got one of those faces which looks as if he's got the
biggest secret in the world. Big black bushy eyebrows. Huge

things. When he screws up his eyes, his whole face hides behind them. Weird. Ainslie says all Sparks are strange. It's because they're not mates or engineers or anything else, really. They don't do anything that anyone else does, so they're always by themselves. Not even the Old Man says much to him.

The Sparks was the radio operator. These were the days of black Bakelite headphones with brown cord plugged into grey broadcast receivers. Round black-faced dials. A man still crouched over a Morse key. Tap, tap, tapping away. Dit-dah-dit-dah. A-A. Dit-dah-dit-dah. Can you hear me? Each ship had to carry a Sparks. That was international law. But he didn't work for the shipping company. His employer was Marconi. Marconi trained operators in Morse code, basic radio maintenance and often typing. That was it. Trained up and then hired out to a ship. Within a few weeks a young man would go from being nobody in Newport to the bridge deck. In the Royal Navy, the radio operator (he wasn't called Sparks; that was an electrician) was a rating. He messed below decks. In merchant ships he was an officer. He wore a peaked cap and a brass-buttoned jacket with two rings on the cuff. He had a good cabin in the officers' quarters. In the old tramp ship his cabin was on the bridge deck, on the starboard side behind the chartroom. His wireless room was on the port side. A swish of the curtain and like Marvo the Magician, the Sparks would slip from bunk to swivel chair in seconds. Weather forecasts. Messages from the owners. Listening out on the quarter-hour for distress signals. Doing things no one else did, or knew how to do. At the end of the trip, back to Marconi's pool, sitting there, waiting for another berth.

It was in Colombo that the Sparks had a little difficulty about his wires. The ship's wireless had to receive signals from relay stations all over the world. No satellites in those days. Aerials were strung from the foremast, back to the mainmast on top of the bridge and then all the way back above number three hatch, above the funnel and the midships accommodation to the top of the after-mast, which supported the big cargo derricks between number four and number five hatch. These aerials were truly the lifelines of the ship and, perhaps, other ships as well, and they were valuable. They were made from copper. In port, the radio operator, the Sparks, took them down. He had to anyway if shoreside cranes were being used because they could easily be in the way of sling crates and bales aboard or ashore. But, once down, these hundreds of feet of pure copper wire were locked away. If they weren't, they'd be stolen. Dockyard thieving was bad in any part of the world. Cargo would always go missing. Cabins were always locked. Scuttles were always clamped tight over portholes even in the hottest climates. An open cabin would be stripped in seconds – even the toothbrush would go – and the booty over the side and ashore. If you wanted your favourite whatever back, then a trip to the local flea market was best – with, of course, your wallet in your pocket and your hand on it, but you'd have to be quick. Back to the aerials in Colombo. Every so often, one or two, maybe all, of the aerials needed replacing. The Sparks did the fixing and mending, but after a time he would have to renew them. So when the ship arrived in port, he'd tell the local Marconi agent and the new wire would be sent aboard. And the old aerials? Officially, they'd be written off. Unofficially, the Sparks would be on first-name terms with all the thieves in all the ports. He'd flog them off. That would set him up for good runs ashore for the next three or four ports and still leave him with some cash left over for a suit at Sam's when they got to Hong Kong. In Colombo, on that trip, this went very wrong.

Sparks has gone ape-shit. Before we got in, Ainslie heard him telling the Mate that he would be renewing all the aerials, including the main, once we were alongside. As usual, we had to take them down. The Sparks does sod all. Just stands there in his whites and his brown sandals his mum sent him telling us to be careful. I mean, how can you be careful with wire? Shitty stuff. Ainslie told him to bog off. He didn't. He never does. Just looks at you under those black eyebrows of his like some Scotch badger. Anyway, when we'd stowed them, the Mate said, Get the hatch boards off numbers two and five and then we can go for a smoke-o. I got two teas from the galley, but Ainslie had disappeared. The Mate came along the starboard gangway and wanted to know where he was. I said he was down aft seeing if the bosun wanted any help. He told me to go for'd and help the casab stow the ropes so these thieving wharfie bastards can't get their hands on them. Job and finish, he said. When I got back to the cabin, Ainslie's sitting there all smug. Wouldn't tell me where he'd been. Thanks a bundle, I said. He told me to belt up and that he'd see me right. That was last night. Didn't know what he meant. This morning, the shit hit the fan. We were up on the boat deck with the Mate when Sparks comes leaping up the after ladder like the sodding Zulus were after him. The bastards have nicked the aerials, he said. He's stomping up and down the deck banging his hands on his sides shouting, Bastards! Bastards! Bastards! The Mate said he should calm down. After all, he was going to renew them anyway. That's the point, says Sparks, I had to change my mind. The agent says he can't get new ones. You mean we've got no aerials, says the Mate. Sparks does some more stomping up and down, but this time he's nodding his head like it's going to fall off. Fucking right, he says. Fucking right. Then they both go off calling the wharfies thieving bastards. I asked Ainslie what happens now, but he didn't say much. Just had his thoughtful look on.

## 6 NOVEMBER 1958, COLOMBO

Course, I should have guessed. Ainslie told me when we got back from a run ashore last night. It was him. He flogged the sodding aerials. He said he didn't see why the Sparks should always get away with it, and if they were being changed it was OK. Anyway, he's got this big wodge of rupees. He said I could have some. Stuff that for a game of soldiers. I don't want it. I'm not getting dropped in the clag when the Mate finds out. I bet he will. He always does. Anyway, I said, what you going to do with all those sodding rupees? No good to anyone. They all want pounds or dollars ashore here. Ainslie said I'm a miserable little turd and if a word of this gets out he'll beat the shit out of me. I don't think we'll ever be close friends.

From Colombo, The Tramp headed south to round Dondra Head and then up into the Bay of Bengal. She was bound for Madras. Another mystery. Another one he'd always thought of as British.

Like a number of youngsters of his generation, whose school history books were, in racing parlance, by Churchill out of *Lives of the Saints*, he had set ideas of what the world looked like and where it was. He also had an unerring notion of his place in it. He was British, and British was best, whether it was motor cars or people. His instincts were born in the eighteenth century. That was a time when the peoples of his islands believed wholly in their Protestant superiority to every race on earth and certainly to the minorities in their own country – the Catholics and Jews especially. The eighteenth-century British believed themselves better than everyone else because they were Protestants. Nothing to do with heavy prayers and steely Christian visions from the Channel ports to wherever Britain petered out into the northern seas. Much simpler: the rest of the world was un-enlightened. Britannia ruled the waves by God's command. James Thomson's lyric was not a claim that Britain rules the waves, but an order from heaven: Britain rule. As the lad's Uncle Harry remarked: Can't say fairer than that. Even in the late 1950s, the lad had learned that Catholics were inferior. They always had lots of children and didn't keep their bathrooms scrubbed. Fundamentally dirty people. Even at Sea Cadets on Wednesday evenings, when it came to prayers, the order was given, 'Fall out the Roman Catholics'. At school, the one Catholic master was pointed out. Roman Catholics didn't attend school assembly. The lad, like his friends, assumed they weren't let off, but weren't let in. There was one Jew at school whom they simply beat up and therefore quite liked. Eventually he left, and so that was that.

Furthermore, the lad had been taught that Britain always won. Even when the Hungarians arrived at Wembley and they didn't, then something was wrong somewhere. Cheated, probably. Whatever. He learned also that when something did go wrong, then the British were gallant (sometimes plucky) losers (just as the Hungarians – repressed, of course – were not brilliant, but plucky winners). Britain could lose so well that, morally, the victors came second. As the old ship opened up the world for him, then the lad began to learn that the British didn't always win. They hadn't even won the war. Now they were about to lose their Empire. That was taking a bit of getting used to because the Empire was his, in his birthright. It was the only thing that made him feel important. It had to. What else did he have? On board, everyone knew what he was and where he came from and he knew his place. Ashore in Sudan, Egypt even a couple of years after Suez, Ceylon and now India, he was white and British. That was enough for even the humblest in his islands to feel superior. His dad talked about fuzzy-wuzzies. His uncle said they were nig-nogs and natives. There was nothing scathing. No hatred, no contempt. That was simply what they were. Collectively, 'darkies'. Whatever fuzzy-wuzzies, nig-nogs and natives were, he wasn't sure. He'd never quite grasped that from their conversations. But one thing he had grasped: whoever or whatever they were, they were 'over there'. Now, he was over there too. He was there with his view of the world based on this imperialist belief that the main features of the great panorama were British. Colonies were not simply ruled by British, they *were* British, just as much as Kent was and, what was more, the natives were proud to stand to attention for the national anthem – the only one they had. The lad never thought any more about this because his own history lessons never taught him anything else. On reflection he might have wondered about it all. But being British, being a lad of the village and having been to school in the 1940s and early 1950s, there was no great reason why he should have thought any differently. Fathers, uncles, the teacher (there was only one) had to be right. After all, no one had ever said they were wrong. So when he left home, he wasn't prepared to be surprised. No one had suggested any different and, truthfully, he knew so little anyway that there was nothing to contradict what he didn't know. He travelled with instinct.

He knew about invaders. So he knew what the Vikings looked like, but had only a vague idea from where they'd come. He remained confused about the Romans. He could never quite match images of the Romans with Italians, who everyone knew always ran away in wars and, when they were caught, changed sides. He'd heard his father and Uncle George laughing that the shortest book in the world was the book of Italian war heroes. The village school had not mentioned Giotto or Rossini. His father had taught him that the only good German was a dead one. The French had been on 'our' side during the war fifteen years before and, in spite of six (maybe eight – he could never remember) hundred years of war, the French were sort of all right and, anyway, we'd always won and Nelson, Wellington and Olivier were heroes. At the same time, somewhere in the back of his mind he felt uneasy about William the Conqueror. The Americans were useless (his father) and wonderful (his mother) and a constant source of chocolate bars and amazing newspaper comic sections (his uncle in New Jersey). The real world, the one that he linked with his history lessons (perhaps more than geography because he switched off at the very mention of escarpments and alluvial plains), was pink and British by right. It was the Empire. The rest, places like China, Russia and South America, of little significance. The big places were British. He may have confused his Nyasalands with his Tanganyikas, but he more or less knew where the Empire was. Some countries were really England. Extensions. Places where he had as much right to walk the streets and ask a policeman what time it was as he did in Bexleyheath or Faversham.

Canada, Australia, New Zealand. Australia was still to his family the same sort of place as was America and England during the late nineteenth century for the Irish. Ten pounds would buy a one-way berth to Sydney, where everyone knew there was opportunity and gangs of them digging for it in the streets. The next most important part of Empire was India. He'd been taught it was no longer British, but the way he was taught and his unremarkable instincts told him that it was. They played cricket, although not at proper Test level.

They all spoke English. Didn't they? The last viceroy was still in the Royal Navy, so it couldn't be that much different. Hardly frock coats ago. He understood that it wasn't Kipling, but they still wore loincloths and had elephants pulling tree trunks, so it was more or less the same. More or less British. Ceylon had been a taster. Brown faces with ivory teeth stained blood-red with betel nuts. Bare hard feet. Beggars and fat cats. Soft saris and starched khaki.

To the lad, Ceylon was the Isle of Wight of India. Now he was in proper India. Proper Raj. So he thought.

## 13 NOVEMBER 1958, MADRAS

We just about got the gangway down at about eight o'clock last night and half the deckhands are ashore. They all knew where to go. The railway lines run on to the wharf. All goods vans. Big maroon or sort of brown. There's a couple of pros in one of them. They don't even slide the waggon doors shut. One of them one end, the other one the other. The deckhands just line up and take their turn. I saw the stand-by quartermaster coming out. No one cheers or anything. The next one in the line just gets up into the waggon. It reminded me of Communion at All Saints. I was on the gangway when a load of the older crew, mostly donkeymen and greasers, started going ashore. All washed and in their best gear. Each one was carrying a bar of pink Sunlight soap. What's going on? The Second Mate looked at me as if I don't know anything. Bagging off, he said. You mean they have a wash afterwards? No. There's some old woman in the end waggon. That's all she charges – one bar of Sunlight for a short time. How do they know? We've only just arrived. They've been coming here for years, he said. Probably the same old woman that gave their fathers one. Don't they get diseases? Oh yes, he said. They'll be poxed up to the eyeballs by the time we sail. Then what happens? The Third Mate gives them a jab. That cures it? Shouldn't think so, he said. Most of them are incurable. Half of them have got a full house anyway. Apparently a full house is gonorrhoea, diarrhoea and pyorrhoea. It sounds pretty grim. I asked the Second Mate why the crew did it if they knew they were going to get the pox. He said it's because they're Chinese. They shag anything that moves or even if it used to, he said. That's why there are so many of them. You wait until we get to China, he said. They're everywhere.

## 15 NOVEMBER 1958, MADRAS

The Flying Angel chaplain came down yesterday morning. Wanted to know if anyone would like to go on a picnic. I asked Ainslie why they organise these things. He said it's to stop us bagging off. He arrived in a small bus and took us to a club by the racecourse. The padre says that a lot of people stayed on after we gave the country back to the Indians. That was ten years ago, he said. One Scottish bloke, who the padre says is an old tea-planter, said that the Indians have made a right cock of it. He says that when we owned it, the Indians were better off because we were fair. He says the Indians aren't fair to each other. He said the whole place is corrupt. Unless you've got a favour owing or a relative, then forget trying to get anywhere. Even the relatives take bribes from each other. I said why did he stay here? He said it was his life. He was born in India and went back to England to school, then came back. He said it's as much his home as it was theirs. When we got back tonight, I told Ainslie about him.

Ainslie said he remembers him from the last trip. Said he was a sad old bugger. Was his wife there? I said I didn't see her. Probably sleeping it off, he said. Sleeping what off? Nostalgia, he said. He said his aunt and uncle were just the same. They'd had to go back to England about ten years ago when the independence thing happened. Now what do they do? He said not much but drink. They live down at a seaside place called Bexhill. He said there's a whole bunch of them in a club. Just sit there, stare at the sea and talk about the good old days. And drink. That's right, he said, mostly drink. Funny thing, he said, the glasses are really cheap and dirty. It was because they'd never had to do the washing-up.

Madras was India's third city. Until 1947 and that hurried independence, it had been British for three centuries. It was the capital of the state with the same name, an area of 142,330 square miles. In the lad's book, they still called it a presidency. Presidency. Goodness knows when the book had been written. The 1920s? Before that? Good enough for The Tramp's library. Why not? It had been more or less good enough for his education. The city, said the book, had a population of 527,000. More like a million. No one cared or noticed that much. The city spread out. The people spread out looking for shade. What they called European Madras had trees enough. The lawns of the British compounds that spread inland and to the south were manicured like the stately homes none of them had in England. Very green. Very cool. Not that much changed. For three hundred years the strengths of Madras had been in trade. Still was. Small coasters sailed and chugged the Bay of Bengal. Maybe to Rangoon. Maybe up to Calcutta. Merchants sent sorghum and coffee, sandalwood and rice, teak and manganese ores. Ashore, there was a fine university. A few grand palaces with tall arches, towers and galleries that won't shudder when the monsoons come. They'd hardly shuddered when the Raj ended. They still pointed to them. Grand monuments like Chepank Palace. It was splendid to Madrasees, unless, that is, they'd been to Bombay or Calcutta. There, they knew how to build palaces. When The Tramp steamed in through the two great breakwaters – there was no proper harbour – the ways of lavish princes had drifted on. Or at least they were supposed to have.

It seemed that twelve years on from independence and partition, great parts of the subcontinent didn't appear to have shaken off the Crown. The day he walked ashore by himself, he felt a mixture of inbred English arrogance and fear.

## 16 November 1958

The place is full of beggars. Sort of brown didicoys. They sit there with their knees bent almost up to their chins with just one skinny arm sticking out. They're quite scary. It's the way they look at you. It's not what I thought it was going to be. But then in some ways it is. I got the *Book of Knowledge* out of the smoke room library. It said that it's a land of red and black. Black cattle along red roads, swarming with little black people with red cloth things instead of shorts. Far as I can see, lot of them have a blob of sort of red lipstick on their foreheads. According to the book, it's religious. Something to do with a god called Vishnu. There's nothing in the book about Vishnu, and the Fourth doesn't know. He said ask the Flying Angel chaplain. I'm not sure about that. Most of them are a bit touchy about religion. The one thing that's everywhere is the heat. It comes off the ground and the walls. No wonder they're all skinny. You wouldn't want to eat much and you're sweating all the time. Ainslie says be sure not to drink local water ashore. So I wonder how they get on. Ainslie says they don't. They've all got the pox or something or other. He says you can run a country ten times better if the water's clean. The Fourth says that his father was out here in the army, and in the afternoon all the colonial servants used to walk up and down on the seafront. He said they were waiting for the breeze. It's called The Doctor. I said I had an auntie who lived in Sidmouth and they did that down there. Ainslie said my auntie was hardly a colonial servant. Probably a charlady. I didn't take any notice. I don't now, but it doesn't stop him. What did shut him up was when I told him about Clive of India. He didn't know that Clive started in India as a clerk in Madras and in fifteen years was governor. He said how did I know? I told him that it was exactly two hundred years ago when I was in Class 4A and we had a talk about it. Ainslie said he didn't believe I was in 4A. More likely 4E. He really won't give over. The Fourth said, Let that be a lesson to you. About what? He said that Clive never made old bones. So much for money. Ainslie said it was probably the climate and drink. Not in Bath, said the Fourth; that's where he did it. Suicide. With a penknife. That shut up Ainslie. The Fourth's brilliant. He must have loads of books, although I've never seen any in his cabin.

## 16 NOVEMBER 1958, MADRAS

I think I know why Ainslie shut up when the Fourth said about Clive committing suicide. We were talking last night about big people not getting so much out of life. He was really quiet for a long time then he said it wasn't just big people. I started to say something about poor people not having much to lose, and he said there was more to it than that. I knew his father was dead. He just said something about him being ill. I wonder if he killed himself? I suppose I could ask the Mate. He would know. I don't want to really. But it would explain why he's so nasty sometimes. Maybe he's just sad. I said a prayer for him, but I'm not sure I should. He doesn't want anyone to be nice to him, except Veronica.

## 17 NOVEMBER 1958

Third Mate came along at smoke-o and asked Ainslie if he fancied a run ashore. Said he'd got an invite from some bloke called Williams to the Railway Institute. He said I could come if I wanted to. Ainslie said I wouldn't want to go because I was probably off to one of the Flying Angel prayer meetings. Third Mate didn't take any notice, just said, Be ready at seven sharp. I asked Ainslie what went on at the Railway Institute. My Scottish uncles always talked about the Railway Athletic Club. Was that it? Ainslie said I'd better not tell them that. The Railway Athletic Clubs are salt and vinegar and mild and bitter in straight glasses. The Madras Railway Institute was different. High-class stuff. Good place to get a wife, he said. A Welsh one? What does that mean, he said. Well, the Third Mate was on about someone called Williams. Ainslie just laughed. You really don't know anything, do you? But he wouldn't say anything else. We'll see.

## 19 NOVEMBER 1958, MADRAS

Now I know about Anglo-Indians. Ainslie calls them 'chee-chees'. It was weird. They're what Dad calls half-castes. Indian and

British. They sound a bit Welsh when they talk, and they use all sorts of words that I thought only boys at posh schools use. Williams said they had a spiffing time at the garden party. Then Mrs Williams said that it was top hole. But it sounds funny because of their accents. There was one man who asked if I played rugger. I told him that I was captain of the Extra As at school. Eton? Not exactly. Harrow? Still, not exactly. I said I was Wilmington. He seemed impressed, but I didn't tell him that the whole village went there except Innis, who was in borstal. Then he wanted to know what did I think of the bah-bahs, or something. I wasn't sure what to say because I hadn't a clue what he was talking about. So I just said I thought they were spiffing and he seemed to agree. As far as I can make out, they've all got English names. The Third Mate said it all started a hundred years ago. Some of the English people out here married Indian women. Really formal.

## 20 NOVEMBER 1958, MADRAS

Third Mate's really nice. He's quite bright and not at all yo-ho-ho stuff. Ainslie says he's a rich ponce. I think that's because he wears suede desert boots on watch and always has peppermint creams. He keeps them in the hospital fridge with all the drugs. He's got the key because he's also the ship's doctor, although I don't think he knows much about it. He had to give one of the deckhands a jab for pox or something and the needle broke off in the poor bastard's arm. Didn't seem to mind too much. Perhaps he thinks that's what happens when you get a jab. The Third Mate rubbed it with a bit of white spirit or something, gave the bugger a peppermint and told him to come back in two days for the second jab. Ainslie says he'd rather his dick fell off than allow the Third Mate near him with a needle. I saw the deckhand the next day and his arm looked like a rugby ball. I asked him if it hurt, and he said, Thank you very much. I told the Fourth this and he said the Chinese are really nice. Very polite. Try sailing with a Liverpool or Glasgow crowd. Not very nice, I asked. 'Very nice? If that had happened to one of them, he'd have knocked seven types of shit out of the Third Mate. It's like sailing with Genghis Khan's in-laws.' I'm not sure what he means, but he made it sound pretty bad.

## 23 November 1958, Cuddalore

Great run ashore. Funny place. We're loading sugar. The local Flying Angel padre organised a cricket match. Ainslie says the padre's a poofter. The Mate says they all are and keep your hand over your bum if he gets you alone. We lost the cricket. Bit strange, really. I thought being English and all that we should have won but the locals were quite good. Afterwards Ainslie and I went with one of them into the village. They call it a town, but it's not as big as Gravesend. But I didn't say anything. We had curry food. Never had it before. Quite liked it. The Mate says I'll have the runs tomorrow.

They really do have bullocks pulling carts. One of them got stuck. There's some little bloke sitting up there beating shit out of the beast with a stick and everyone laughing. But they seem nice enough. There was one strange thing that we found. There are only two proper streets and in the middle of the sort of high street was a Bata shoe shop. There's one in Bexleyheath, so I suppose they're right. It is a town.

\* \* \*

Now began one of the oddest voyages of all. A circumnavigation of the globe – and just one cargo.

# 11

## THE CIRCUMNAVIGATION

The Tramp sailed from India on to Hong Kong, this time for a couple of repairs and a crew change. The owners had fixed her to sail to Cuba and load sugar for China. Long enough trip. Long way to go from Hong Kong to fetch a cargo. But times were harder than before, and in theory it should have been a simple enough trip. Bunkers in Hawaii, through Panama, load in Havana, then south of the island and Cueba Hueca by Santiago and back through to Shanghai. They'd make a shilling or two out of it.

But on 1 January 1959, that sort of thing stopped being simple. That was the day that President Batista fled from Havana and a pretty good baseball player (and an even better revolutionary) by the name of Fidel Castro took over. Washington had Commies in its back yard. The Tramp was about to load Commie sugar and take it to Commie China. Chance to prove something.

## 15 December 1958

This is going to be a long trip. It won't end until next year. Long before we got to the first stop, I'll have been at sea for a year and never been home. This time, we're going all the way round. Right round the world. The Mate says that because we're going to Cuba, the Americans won't let us bunker in Hawaii. What's it got to do with them? He says it's McCarthy, the senator who hates Communists. I said I thought he died last year. Anyway, so what? The Mate says the whoo-er may be dead but that doesn't stop the Yanks hating the Reds. I told him that Dad said the Russians were on our side during the war. (I didn't tell him Mum calls Dad a socialist bleeder especially when he sits in the kitchen playing 'The Red Flag' on his ukulele.) The Mate said the Russkies were on their own side. Everyone is. He said the Americans reckon the bloke that took over a couple of months ago in Cuba – someone called Castro – is a Communist. This means that we can't go to Hawaii because that's American and why should they help the Cubans? I said that they'd be helping us. He said I'd soon learn.

So we've got to go all the way across the Pacific to Vancouver and take bunkers there, probably Coos Bay again, and then down to the Panama Canal, then through that to Havana. But once we've been to Havana, the Americans won't let us back through the Canal. I didn't know that was theirs as well. Perhaps the whole world belongs to America. That's what the Fourth says. It used to be ours; now it's theirs. That means we have to sail across the Atlantic, bunker at Gib or maybe even Ceuta, because that's Spanish and they don't mind – but they might by the time we get there – through the Med, then Suez again, down the Red Sea, bunker at Aden, across the Indian Ocean (where we've just come from), bunker at Singapore, then up to Shanghai. Something's potty somewhere. All we're doing is taking a couple of bags of sugar to China. Fourth says the Yanks are very touchy. They'll have probably bombed Cuba to sugar lumps by the time we get there. If we do. He says there's a big conspiracy in the world and that Churchill was right. What about, I said. He gave me his constable's look and said, About everything. He then strode off in a southerly direction along the engineers' gangway. In other words, he doesn't know either. I suppose the company's got this worked out. Someone must be paying a fortune for this cargo.

## 19 DECEMBER 1958

Here we go again. The casab doesn't speak much English and he gets on my nerves. The other morning I went into the fo'c's'le and I was singing 'The Deadwood Stage'. I don't know many of the words, but I always liked the bit where Calamity Jane sings, 'Hi, Joe, where d'you get them fancy clothes?'. That's what I was singing. So the casab says, What this hi-joe belong? I didn't say anything at first. Best to ignore him. But he has to give you stores for everything. So after a bit he's at it again. What this hi-joe where joe get them fancies clothes belong? Or something like that. So I said it was a sort of greeting. I no before hear this fashion, he says. So I told him it was really smart English. I didn't think any more about it. That was Friday forenoon. Apparently, when the Old Man and Mate went round on Captain's rounds on Sunday forenoon, the Old Man walks in with his full uniform and the sodding casab says to him, Hi Joe where d'you get them fancy clothes. Well, apparently the Old Man is sort of upset and afterwards the casab tells the Mate that I told him to say it. I said

I was sorry and that I'd apologise to the Old Man. The Mate said he'd have my guts for garters if I tried to. I bet he doesn't explain. Ainslie says it'll look brilliant on my voyage report. He says I'll be lucky to get a job as a greaser on a London Greek after this.

## CHRISTMAS DAY 1958, NORTH PACIFIC

Doesn't seem like Christmas Day. No carols. No holly. No church service. Just a nasty force eight three points on the starboard quarter. She's been rolling like a bugger for three days. Steward came in with the soup just as she gave an extra-big one. Zoom! Out he goes with empty soup-plates looking for a cloth and muttering 'djuny-er' which I think is Chinese for 'frig it'. The stewards sprinkle water on the tablecloths to make the plates stick, which is OK if the ship would keep still. One second you're leaning right across for your soup, the next it's heading straight for you. Sparks said it's all good practice for him when he sails round the world. Not forgetting Papeete, Tahiti, I said. He tapped his nose and gave one of his winks. Just wait, he said, Just wait. I expect he's sent another letter to the mayor.

It would have been nice to get a few cards. Couple of people got messages. No one said what they were. I suppose it's private. Missing you and all that stuff. I was lying in my bunk this morning thinking about home. I'm not sure what I see now. We've been away for more than eight per cent of my life. I've had five letters. I suppose it's my fault. I've more or less stopped writing. Once a port and that's it. There isn't much to say. I suppose it's because I don't much belong there any more.

## 13 January 1959, Vancouver

Got a letter. Mum and Dad are going to live in Australia. They say there's not much for them in England. They didn't say anything about me going with them. I suppose after all this time they assume that I don't live there any more. I suppose they're right. But it would be nice to go home and see my things. I hope they don't throw them away when they go. I wonder where I'll go on leave? Never thought of them not being there. Odd. You can feel homesick when you start thinking there may not be a home. That must be what homesickness really is. Not longing for something that's there, but longing for something that you had, that used to be there.

## 14 January 1959, Vancouver

We've got a new Captain. And we've got a Mrs Captain. The other Captain's gone to another ship because their skipper's died. Sparks said he thinks he may have fallen overboard. Mrs Captain is very pretty. The Fourth says everyone will have to watch their language. The Chief said it's not right having women on board. It's unlucky. The Second Mate said he wished he had one, especially if she looked liked the Captain's wife. That, said the Chief, is exactly what he was talking about. Women on ships are trouble. Fourth said they're trouble anywhere. At least that was something everyone agreed on.

## 18 January 1959, off California

New Captain's really nice. He came down to our accommodation when I was practising last night. I thought I was going to get a bollocking. He said he wanted me to know that he and Herself (that's what he calls his wife) really like my playing. The trumpet's their favourite instrument. Ainslie couldn't believe it. He hates it. So he told the Captain that I did requests. Can you play 'Oh My Papa'? Ainslie said of course I could and I would play it that very evening. I stood in the heads playing it because the acoustics are brilliant. Ainslie kept frigging about in front of me trying to make me laugh. It's pretty difficult to spit down a brass tube in tune while Ainslie's trying to put you off. When I saw the Captain this morning, he said thank you very much, but he didn't ask me to play anything else. I might give it a rest for a couple of days. Anyway, we'll be alongside tonight. Wonder what it's like? I think Cuba's the first place we've been to that wasn't British. I know America isn't but it was a long time ago and they are on our side in things.

## 9 FEBRUARY 1959, HAVANA

Havana is wonderful. It smells great. The whole town, maybe the whole island, smells of cigars. Cigars in the sun. Cigars at night. It must be the place to smoke them. The people are nice. Easygoing. Ainslie and I went to a bar last night. Really warm. We had Cuba libres. Rum and Coca-Cola. Lots of music. Trumpets and guitars. Never thought of them going together. But they do. The Fourth said I should bring my trumpet ashore and join in. Wouldn't be any good. These people play a C-trumpet. It's high-pitched with different fingering, I think. Great stuff to listen to. And the señoritas are really pretty. Better than the lot in the Cherry Bar in Hong Kong. In Hong Kong they were all called

Suzie Wong. Here they're all Carmen or Rosa or something like that.

## 11 FEBRUARY 1959, HAVANA

I was in a bar last night with the Third Mate. It's near a place called the Capitolio, which I think is their sort of Parliament. I told the Fourth about it. He said Parliament is stretching a point in this place, which is full of Commie bastards. I said, What was here before? He said, Mafia bastards.

On the walls of the bar are pictures of people the Third Mate says are very famous. But the most famous one of all is Ernest Hemingway. I've read a couple of his books and they're tremendous, especially *For Whom the Bell Tolls* and the *Old Man and the Sea*, which I think happened here. I can't make out if he still lives here or used to. The barman said I was sitting on his stool. Maybe I'll be a writer one day. At least I'm seeing things, which is good for any writer, and I quite like Bacardi.

The barman reckons this Castro who took over last month is good news. I said the Americans don't think so. He said that Americans don't like anyone except Americans and anyway it's better not to talk like that. Things are different now.

He said that Castro gave a speech the other day from the steps of the Capitolio and he went on for five hours. Wonder what took five hours to say? Auntie Kitty in Scotland talks all the time, but not for five hours. No one would listen to her for five hours. Not even Uncle Bill, who does as he's told most of the time. No wonder he does a lot of overtime. But these Cubans just have to stand there. They can't go home in the middle of it otherwise they get arrested. I suppose that's what happens in revolutions.

Somebody has one so the people can be free, then tells the people whom they've rescued from the other lot exactly what they've got to do. These Cubans go about shouting 'Viva!' quite a lot. I'm not sure what they're Viva-ing if they've got to stand around for five hours listening to this Castro.

The barman said that his mother, who lives in the middle of the island, reckons she's going to have a fridge. Isn't that good? He says, yes, very good. But she's got no electricity. Viva!

## 14 FEBRUARY 1959, HAVANA

Had to take one of the quartermasters to the hospital. Very pretty street with lots of trees. But there's not much in the hospital. I got talking to two blokes who don't look much older than me. They said they are doctors and they're short of everything. It's going to get worse, they said. One of them said could I help them get off the island? I said, Why not just go? He said, You can't do that now. I asked him how long he'd been a doctor. He said he was in his second year. As a doctor? No, just a medical student. And he was supposed to be looking after Fan Kan. He said a lot of doctors got out while they could. So why is everyone Viva-ing? He said, Not everyone is, but anything's better than Batista.

## 15 FEBRUARY 1959, HAVANA

This is a scary place. There was a guard by the gangway. He looked straight out of some dago film. Highly pressed khaki drills and then everything else black. Black slick hair, black eyes, black moustache, black belt, black holster, black boots. It was the gun that gave me the willies. I was on gangway-watch with the quartermaster – the cocky one with the smashed watch. He's maybe cocky, but he speaks Spanish. He said he worked in South America. Maybe. Anyway, every so often he would yell something down to the guard and the guard starts showing off. First it's nothing special. Does the important walk up and down. Picks on a couple of wharfies and makes them show their papers or something. All the time he's giving a quick look to see if we're watching. Next thing he's got his gun out and sliding the chamber and things. The quartermaster calls him a cowboy, *caballero* or something. Stupid! The guard looked round really quick, and the next thing the sodding gun goes off and there's a wanging sound in the bulkhead right by us. The quartermaster and me hit the deck, but it was all over by then. The first thing I see is the Mate's beard sticking out of his port wanting to know what the fuck's going on, Chuck? From where I was lying in the scuppers, not much. Course, now the Captain's got to make a formal complaint to the agent. There's going to be trouble. I just know there is. Ainslie, of course, is really helpful. He said it was my fault for letting the quartermaster shout things. I said, Thanks a bundle, I nearly got killed. Oh, says Ainslie, aren't we just the hero? Pity I didn't get a bullet up my bum. Problem is, in a way Ainslie's right. I should have told the quartermaster to pack it in. This isn't an ordinary place. But I don't like ordering people about.

## 18 FEBRUARY 1959, CUEBA HUECA

The new skipper is very relaxed. We cleared Havana and sailed around here to Cueba Hueca. We've had to anchor. There's not much water and they're going to bring the sugar out in barges. This will take ages to load. The locals are in no hurry. Anyway, once we'd anchored, the Captain said to the Mate, 'Well, that seems all right then. All went very well. Will you be so kind as to have the motorboat lowered. My wife and I are off for a few days.'

The Mate knows him of old. Seems he always does this. Gets into port and shoots off to a hotel somewhere with Mrs Captain and leaves the Mate in charge. You wouldn't think a place like this had a hotel. The Mate says it's some way inland and there's no telephone. Goodness knows what happens if we finish loading ahead of schedule. We'll simply have to sit at anchor and wait until the pair of them turn up.

I was on boat-duty with the Third Mate and we ran them ashore. Naturally I got lumbered with having to carry their suitcases up the beach to the Chevrolet they'd organised. I said I hoped they had a good a time. At first he looked at me as if he was surprised that I spoke English. Then he said, I imagine we will.

Ainslie says he probably thought I was trying to get a tip.

## 26 February 1959, At Sea

Sighted some people in an open boat at first light. I was on watch with the Mate and spotted them off the starboard bow. We stopped ship, but the Captain said not to lower a ladder until we saw who they were. They looked rough. The boat was pretty scruffy and they'd taken on a bit of water, but they hadn't got any to drink. They're Cubans. Four of them. Two young blokes and two old blokes. Trying to escape to Florida. The cocky quartermaster talked to them in Spanish. They wanted us to take them to Miami. The Captain said no. But we lowered six quite big water bottles and some bread. One of them started making smoking signs. The Mate told the chief steward to get a carton of Lucky Strikes. Who pays? The Mate was disgusted and told him to get on with it. The Second Mate said they've got a reasonable chance as long as the weather holds. It's only ninety miles across. They'll have to take their chances, he said. At least they won't be thirsty. Made me think about the two medical students. You have to be desperate to take your chances out here. Sun. Sharks. Shot at if the Cubans find you. Arrested if the Americans see you. Run down at night if another ship doesn't.

## 27 FEBRUARY 1959, AT SEA – JUST!

Near miss last night. We were doing ten knots on our way to Nassau for bunkers. Bit misty, but nothing much. Out of nowhere comes this cruise ship. More lights than New York. I reckon she was no more than a hundred yards off, which is not much when you think we're half as much as that again. Loads of horn blasting. How come she didn't see us? We could see the radar scan going around. The Third Mate says it was a dago boat. The officer of the watch was probably giving the steward one on the chartroom table. We couldn't see anything, of course. No radar on this thing. People ashore think we've all got it. We haven't. In London they say we don't need radar. We'd just get lazy and rely on it and never keep a proper lookout. We were keeping a proper lookout last night.

## 3 MARCH 1959, ATLANTIC BOUND FOR GIBRALTAR

Had a session on ship construction and engineering this

morning. Not sure I understand it, but I like the idea. The Fourth was supposed to be telling us about our lot. Steam reciprocating, that's all he kept saying. I think they try to make it complicated just to hide how simple it is. There's a diagram of a ship called the *Cairncross* in the book. It says that it was the first cargo ship with geared turbines and that the turbines were built by Parsons of Newcastle in 1912. This is special. My grandfather worked on those engines in 1912 at Parsons. I told the Fourth. He said I was a cocky bugger and maybe I thought I should be doing the lesson and not him. Ainslie says the Fourth knows bugger all. He used to be an engineer before the war then became a copper. Now he's retired, he's come back just to see the world. Ainslie says he couldn't get a job on the Woolwich ferry except that he's a Mason.

## 15 MARCH 1959, GIBRALTAR

I reckon I'm really lucky to be alive. I think we all are. We were coming through the Strait of Gibraltar last night. Very, very foggy. Engines on Slow Ahead. Long blasts on the ship's whistle [hooter]. I went on watch at four this morning and was sent for'd as fo'c's'le lookout. You stand right up for'd on a metal platform in the bows. There's a bell with a clapper. The Mate said that if you see anything on the starboard bow then you hit the bell once. On the port bow you hit it twice, and if anything's ahead then you hit it three times. That way the bridge will look in the direction rather than you shouting and not being understood. I got up on the fo'c's'le and it was so dense that when I looked back I couldn't even see the bridge properly. We were hardly moving through the water. Then we blew two blasts, which meant that the engines were stopped and we weren't making any headway. We kept on signalling this. I think it was lucky we weren't moving. Or maybe if we had been, the tanker would have missed us. There were foghorns everywhere, but we couldn't see any other ships. Then I heard engines, but I couldn't see her and I wasn't even sure where they were coming from because the fog distorts everything. There's no bell signal for that. So I yelled back at the bridge: Engines! Engines! Suddenly from nowhere this huge tanker is coming at us on the port bow. As I rang the bell I could see we were going to hit so I ran for the ladder. I jumped it. I was just landing on the main deck when I heard someone shouting from the bridge: Clear the fo'c's'le! Got something right, I thought. At the same time I could hear the bridge telegraph ringing. It must have been Full Astern. The whole ship was shuddering, but we hadn't even moved when . . . Bang! We hit. Next thing I'm up in the air, then on my backside sliding across the deck, luckily into the hatch coaming and not the other way, which would have been over the side. All I could think of was, Please, God, make her fully laden. Please. Please. If the tanker had been light ship [empty], she could have exploded. She was full.

I got up to the bridge. It was very calm. The Captain didn't look at all worried. Seems he'd said all the right things. Second Mate had stayed on the bridge and was talking to the Chief on the engine room telephone. The Mate was on his way for'd with the bosun. Sparks was reporting our position to Gib – as best we knew it. Chippie was already out of his bunk and sounding the tanks. The stand-by quartermaster had made the tea. The Captain even had time to ask if I was OK. Ainslie said later that it's a wonder I hadn't asked him if he'd like me to play 'For Those in

Peril', in the key of C so everyone could join in. I think we were all a bit tense.

Then suddenly the fog lifted. There's the tanker with a huge black metal plate (ours) sticking out amidships. There's us with a sodding great hole in the bow. There's the Rock of Gibraltar. There's me, all in one piece.

## 17 MARCH 1959, GIBRALTAR

We're alongside in Gib having the bow fixed – more or less, as the Mate says. We're filling the lower forepeak with cement and then welding plates over the hole. It'll get us through to Shanghai, and then we can dry-dock in Hong Kong. Well, I hope it does. The Fourth says he wouldn't let some dago repair the ship. From his experience with the Spaniards, or so he says, they couldn't repair a pair of boots without stealing half the tacks. He's a gloomy sod, but they don't look too bright.

This should be an easy time, but it isn't. All the stores are in the fo'c's'le. We have to take it in turns sitting below watching the workmen in case a spark from their welding torches sends up the million gallons of kerosene and paint that we've got down there. The other reason is to make sure the bastards don't steal any of the million gallons or anything else they can get their hands on. The Mate says that all Spaniards are thieving bastards. They seem nice enough. But it's best to assume he's right. All the time there's a huge hole just above the waterline, I suppose it would be easy to bring a boat alongside at night and have everything out and ashore before anyone saw them. Talking of ashore, the Captain and Mrs Captain are off again. Bridal suite in the Rock Hotel. The Mate says they've had more honeymoons than the Gabor sisters.

*  *  *

There's something about arriving in port for the second time. The first visit to Gibraltar was for bunkers. Just a few hours. This time The Tramp was out on one of the harbour walls. Plenty of time for runs ashore. Plenty of time to see if that silk shop really was as good as it looked first time when there was just an hour ashore before the bunker tubes were let go and engines rung to Stand-By. The Suez Canal again. De Lesseps, a still and fallen idol. This time pleased to see the gully-gully man as if he were an old friend, not a rogue who'd pick a pocket while a lad stood mesmerised by day-old chicks. The bumboatman in long brown coat clambered aboard with inlaid musical cigarette boxes and Spanish fly and greeted him like a brother: Hey, Johnny, nice to see you again. Feeling familiar comradeship even though the lad knew that last time through, that first time through, the patter had been the same. Always the same. Hey, Johnny, nice to see you again. Always nice to see you again, even for the first time. Every time was new. He was growing older. Growing up. Didn't have to be told to lock the cabin, screw down the deadlights. Remember to buy a film with the camera. Better not to buy the camera. He'd been south. Didn't know it, but he was different. Still naive. He'd always be that. But no longer nervous about it.

Going through the Canal that night, passing the ghosts of Ismailia to starboard, came the dawning. He'd not simply done this before. He'd gone right round the world to do it. A real circumnavigation. Right round. Drake in a tramp. Something very special. As he stood out on the wing of the bridge, he gently patted the varnished dodger as a shepherd might his collie after a long and good drive. All the way round. Except for one moment of defiance, his world would have been a street corner. Where else would he have learned about banging a chunk of wood in a ship's side to stop it sinking?

## 14 April 1959, Indian Ocean

We've got a hole in the hull. Chippie was sounding tanks this morning. All dry as a parson's armpit (that's what the Second Mate said) except number three tank. It's full of water. There's a hole in the side. The Second Mate thinks the whole thing's a scream. He says it's all to do with pooping and pissing beasts.

A couple of trips ago, they had a part-cargo of mules. (The Mate says this old thing would carry one-legged budgies if the owners thought they could make a bob out of it.) They kept these mules in the 'tween decks, that's the sort of half-deck between the top of the hatch and the main part of the hold. Well, according to the Second Mate all these mules ever did was eat, piss and poop which, when you come to think of it, was all there was for the poor sods to do. So the problem was obvious. How do you muck out mules down a hold in a ship? The answer was to hose down the 'tween deck and have a series of drain cocks in the side of the ship. Hose them down. Open the drain. The poop and piss run into the sea. Shut the drain cock valves. All tickety-boo. When the mules were put ashore, the drain cocks were taken out and plates welded over the holes. But it seems that when we went into Taikoo dry dock and the hull was chipped and scraped for painting, one of the coolies stuck a chipping hammer through one of the plates and didn't mention it. So we go pounding through a gale and the hole gets worse and the water's inboard instead of in the sea where it should be.

When we got the corner hatch boards off you could see the problem. The sea water had washed over the bags of sugar, the sugar had turned to molasses and most of it on the starboard side had run out of the hole or down into the bilges. And did it pong!

Bagged sugar stinks anyway, but this is revolting. The trouble is, the hole is under the 'tween deck frame and we can't get at it from the inside.

The Mate says someone has to go over the side and put a bung in it. Ainslie immediately told him that I'd love to do it. In the middle of the sodding Indian Ocean, which as everyone knows is full of sharks, killer whales and giant manta rays. It's a wonder Ainslie didn't suggest they threw me in so that someone else could fix the rotten bung while the sharks were distracted fighting over what was left of me. Then the Third said something about there being more sharks on board than over the side, and Ainslie had to say that he was right and that most of them were in the engineers' alleyway. I don't mind having to do it, not if I'm tied on properly. What bothers me is that if I don't get the banging in right, then the water will still come in and who knows what happens then. We've had enough excitement with holes and near holes for one trip.

## 16 APRIL 1959, HEADING FOR CEYLON

The Mate did it. Ainslie says it was only because I would have made such a cock of it. I asked him why he hadn't volunteered. He said he had nothing to prove. Fact is the Mate wouldn't let anyone else go over. Too dangerous he said. Personally I think that's rubbish. She may be rolling about a bit, but as long as you're tied on, the worst you can do is drop the sodding hammer. What a ship! Cement in the bows. Bit of tin welded on the front. A bung amidships just, but only just, above the waterline.

## 17 April 1959, South of the Bay of Bengal

Abeam Dondra Head at midnight just as I came on watch. Picked up the loom of the light twenty miles off. It's quiet now, but we picked up a big electric storm from somewhere. Sparks says there was nothing on the forecast. Last time we were off Dondra, we went north into the Bay of Bengal and Madras. I'm not in a big hurry to go back there, but I'd like to get to Colombo again. Nice people heading for war is what the Flying Angel padre said. I hope not. Good cricketers.

## 22 April 1959, Malacca Strait

Into the Malacca Strait (everyone says Malacca Straits. It's not, it's Strait. Says so in the Pilot Book) during the night. I'm glad I was on watch. We're quite close and it's good to be taking bearings. I quite like coasting. Makes everything more interesting. But it's the smell that's amazing. You can smell the vegetation and the rainforests. It's like being in Pop's greenhouse when all the tomatoes are up. Wonder how everyone is?

## 28 April 1959, South China Sea

Blowing a hooley. Life raft on the Old Man's starboard deck carried away on the twelve to four last night. I was on the wing looking down at her. We'd had green ones coming over the side for two hours solid. But it wasn't a wave that did it. The wind. One of the fittings was loose. The Second Mate told me to go and see if I could get a lashing on her. The only handy rope was up in the fog locker on the monkey island. The quartermaster said, Too dangerous to go topsides, sir. Is it buggery, said the Second Mate. It took me about twenty minutes to get up there and back. When I got down again, the Second Mate looked a bit worried and asked if I was all right. Course I wasn't, but I wasn't going to tell him so that he could tell the whole ship in the morning that I'd chickened out. Anyway, I was just going down the ladder to the Old Man's deck when the raft broke from the for'd lashing. I thought I was going with her. There's no protection from anything down on that deck. You can see all the way to sodding China, and the way the wind was going I was about to be blown there. The thing was hanging over the side when another big gust took her clean away. I was frightened out of my skin. All the time I'm thinking about the sodding bow. What happens if the Fourth was right about the Spaniards? What happens if the sodding front end falls off? The Second Mate was bawling (he's one of life's bawlers) to come back up to the bridge. I couldn't move. Without realising it, I'd lashed myself to the handrail. When I got back to the bridge, the Old Man was there. He wanted to know what the frigging heck I was doing down on the boat deck. Wanted to know if I was out of my frigging mind and what the frigging heck did I think I could do in that wind? I looked at the Second Mate, but he didn't say anything. Thanks very much, sir.

## 30 APRIL 1959, SOUTH CHINA SEA

This is the first time I've had a chance to write anything. The wind's blown through, or at least the worst of it. There are still big seas and we're all in wet-weather gear, but it's nothing like the past couple of days. The chief steward said he thought we were going down. The chippie says it's a typhoon. I didn't think typhoons happened at this time of year. Oh yes, says Chippie, this wind belong typhoon. Very good Chinese word, he says. According to him it's ta-fong – big wind. It's really strange. I reckon I should have been even more frightened than I was. The ship was all over the place. The quartermaster and the stand-by quartermaster were both on the wheel. The Second Mate said I had to stay on watch because no one else could get up to the bridge from the midships accommodation. Chippie's ta-fong was really blowing like stink right up our chuff and we couldn't get into it. She'd ride really high and then dip. I looked astern and there was this humungous sea coming straight down. It was really miles bigger than us. Tall as a building. You didn't just look at it. You had to put your head back to see the top. I thought it was going to land right on top and that would be that. But when it arrived it seemed to go right under, lift us up, then rush by and ahead. The stern went up as if we were going to nose-dive to the bottom, and you could hear, even in all the storm noise, that the screw was out of the water and screaming like hell because it had no water to get a grip in. The Second Mate said he didn't think it could be like this with a ship our size. We're 7,000 tons and 425 feet long. We may be an old tramp steamer, but we're still a fair size. No yacht. The Old Man told Sparks to report our position every half-hour and then to stand by in the radio room just in case. Just in case what? If anything went wrong, no one was going to find us. So why wasn't I scared witless? My Aunt Betts always said it was best to be big and brave when there was trouble. But it wasn't that. I just felt that nothing was going to happen. It wasn't like being in a scow or the barge. When the wind gets up, then you're pretty close and you can get scared all you like, but the best thing is to get on with things. Work the sheets, take a couple of reefs in the mains'l. But in this ship there's a feeling of being on equal terms. I know big ships go down, but somehow I just knew we'd be OK. I don't know what anyone else thinks. No one has said anything. But I knew everything was OK this morning when the Second Mate complained that the baked beans weren't very good and the steward said these were new ones. How the Second Mate knew, I don't know. They tasted the same to me – especially in that weather.

It's Mum's birthday again. I wonder how old she is? Odd I don't know. Don't know when Dad was born either. Don't know when they were married. Or how they met. In fact, I don't know anything about them. I wonder what they know about me?

## 1 MAY 1959, AT SEA

We shall be in Shanghai in a couple of days. China proper. I wonder what old Birchell [his geography master] would say about that? He reckoned I was useless at geography. That was because he never told us about anything but rainforests and rotten alluvial plains. Hardly anything about places and people. I don't think he knew anything. Look it up, that's all he ever said. I thought we could ask you, sir. I thought you'd already looked it up. That's why you've got the gown thing. He sent me outside then. Made me stay there for the rest of the term. But I wish I knew about China. All this way and I don't really know what happens here. The Mate said, Have a look in the ship's library. Fat chance. There's not much in there. I've looked. Wish Dad had let me bring my books.

The ship's library in the old tramp was nothing more than a glass-fronted bookcase with four or five shelves holding maybe a hundred books. Pretty dull. Two copies of *Northanger Abbey*. *Mr Midshipman Easy*. *The Badminton Library Cricket*. *Portuguese Voyages, 1498–1663*. *The Serpent and the Staff*. *Cassell's Book of Knowledge* complete with a fat volume of Index. Assorted good works. Not a steamy scene in any one of them. There had been a copy of *How the Human Body Works*, but the Chief Engineer (a Wee Free) took it on himself to remove it. Not the sort of thing for a long voyage and, if anyone really wanted to know, then he, the Chief, would give freely of his opinion. After all, he had a Chief's Steam Ticket and Diesel Endorsement and so knew everything about pumps and plumbing which, as far as he was concerned, was all any self-respecting sailor needed to know about the human body. So the book was removed and never seen again. What the Chief did with it was never clear.

## 2 MAY 1959, AT SEA

The Fourth seems to know most things. He's got loads of books. He won't let you look at them, but he'll tell you things. I suppose what he says is right. All those books, he must be. He just says, Come and ask. So I do. Ainslie says the Fourth doesn't really know anything, he just looks it up. What's wrong with that, I said. It's knowledge without knowing anything more than you've read, he said. Maybe he's got something. A couple of times I've asked the Fourth things and he hasn't known.

I think it's interesting that no one on board knows much about China. There's Hong Kong and the Korean War stuff, and everyone knows about mandarins, pigtails and long fingernails up their sleeves. But they don't know much more. The Mate was talking about the Great Wall of China. I asked where it was. He said what did I mean, where was it? China, of course. I said, What bit of China? Across, he said. Does that mean it's everywhere? I could see I was pushing my luck a bit and so didn't say anything more. Nor did the Mate, so that proves it. No one except the Fourth really knows anything, and he only knows what he's read, and if he hasn't read all the way down the page then when you ask him questions he doesn't really know the answers. Maybe that's what they mean when they talk about Life. If you read all the way down the page then you might get to know what it is.

## 3 MAY 1959, OFF SHANGHAI

We're having to wait for a pilot before we can go upriver. The Second Engineer reckons his great-grandfather came here on the first voyage of a clipper called the *Cutty Sark*. Wooden ships and iron men, according to him. He knows I spent a bit of time on the Thames. When I told him no engine, just sail, the others reckoned it was bullshit. He told them to pipe down. Interesting how he's got respect for sailormen. Must be his great-grandfather. In the blood.

## 4 MAY 1959, SHANGHAI

We came up the river this morning. Big panic on. Anyone who's got a camera has to give it to the chief steward and he has to put it in the bond store. Mate says the Chinese think we're all spies. If anyone even has a camera on them, they'll take them ashore to the pokey. He says there are three British seamen in the jail. They got a lot of small gunboats, but nothing smart as far as I can see. Mate says not to argue. Just do it and behave yourself. When we came alongside there were hundreds of them. You wouldn't need a winch. They do it all by hand. I threw a messenger* and about six of them caught it. Next thing the head-rope's going out like a flash of pig's wotsit. I waved at them, but they just stared at me. Maybe they're not allowed to smile. The immigration people came aboard as soon as we were tied up. All in these army uniforms with red edges and funny little hats. They reckoned my jabs aren't up to date. Course they are. I had them done in London. The Third Mate's dealing with it. But they didn't take any notice of him either. I had to have the lot done. Next thing this Chinaman's got something the size of a bike pump and stabbing it in my arm. I thought he was trying to nail my arm to my friggin' ribs. I don't know what they put in there, but my left arm's the size of one of Pop's marrows. Mate wouldn't let me ashore. Thanks a bundle, Mr Wong.

## 5 MAY 1959, SHANGHAI

The Second Engineer has got a snake in his cabin. It didn't sneak in. They're friends.

## 6 MAY 1959, SHANGHAI

The Chinese are having a go at the Mate. They say it's his fault that a lot of the sugar's gone. They reckon they're not going to sign for the cargo, only part-cargo. We've had to get all the spoiled bags out, count them and stack them. They get subtracted from

*A thin line which is easy to throw ashore. The ship's end is attached to the heavy mooring rope. Someone ashore catches the messenger, wraps it about a drum and so pulls ashore the thick mooring rope.

the cargo tally. They're not going to like this in London.

## 7 MAY 1959, SHANGHAI

Arm's still swollen. Mate sent me ashore to see the agent's doctor.
The agent's runner came on board to collect me. You'd miss him
in a crowd of two. He's got some blue jacket buttoned right up to
the neck and a blue cap. They all look like their president or
whatever he is, Chairman Mao. His picture's everywhere. Some
of the pictures are twenty or thirty feet tall. Big buildings have
one wall completely covered with a picture of this chap. Brilliant
painting. It can't be just one artist. The Fourth says they're very
good at doing teacups and small black boats on moonlit lakes.
There's something very odd about this chap's face. He's got this
humungous wart. Enormous. When it's halfway up the side of a
skyscraper it must be three feet across. Imagine having a wart that
big. You'd think they'd do something about it. I suppose that's
what makes him different. They all look the same, but he's the
one with the wart.

Walked through the gardens by the river. There's a notice
saying: CHINESE AND DOGS NOT ALLOWED. The agent's runner,
whose name is Chiu (I think), says it's a reminder of how badly
they were treated by the British. I said that was a load of bollocks.
This place was really doing well when we were here. He pointed
to the notice again and said, You velly bad for Chinese. I said,
What about the *Amethyst*?* He said he knows nothing about that.

*HMS *Amethyst* was trapped in the Yangste River and shelled by Communist Chinese
artillery. The Captain was killed. The frigate ran the gauntlet of this bombardment
for 140 miles. The first the British knew that the *Amethyst* had escaped was when a
signal was received from the ship: 'Have rejoined the fleet south of Woosung. No
damage or casualties. God save the King.'

I said that he must. I was only six then, but I know. I told him, Everyone knows; it was on the front page of the *Daily Express*. He must have seen it. But he said nothing more and then pretended he didn't speak English.

## 9 May 1959, Shanghai

The Fifth Engineer's got constipation. Why we should have to know beats me. He says he had it once before when he was in the Navy. The Third Mate says he's not surprised. In the Navy they get all sorts of things stuck up their bums. I think that's unfair. I like the Fifth. He's quiet and quite old. The Third Mate is supposed to be the ship's doctor, or at least he's in charge of the medical locker. He found some really foul stuff and told the Fifth that he had to take it four times a day. I asked the Third Mate what it was. He said he wasn't sure but the list said it was OK for typhoid. He said he reckoned it had to be strong enough to give the Fifth the runs.

## 11 May 1959, Shanghai

The longest bar in the world is here, and I've leaned on it. It's very wide and dark wood down one side of this room that's nearly the size of a football pitch – well, at least half a one. Once it was called the Shanghai Club. Now it's just the seamen's club. It used to be the posh club for all the foreigners who owned Shanghai a few years ago. Some of the things they had are special and some of it is still here. The Fourth said that the bar has very rare French brandy. He said they're gradually bringing it up from the cellars and using it up. So, he says, you go to the bar, order a brandy and they serve it just like in a pub for hardly anything at all. Just a few pennies. We tried it. I suppose it's good stuff. I said I liked beer best. He said I'd get used to it. He said anyone would at these prices. The Fourth says a bottle of the stuff would cost him hundreds of pounds in London. He said the French red wine is better and beats some of the best in Paris. I asked Ainslie how the Fourth would know about this sort of thing. After all, he's only a Fourth Engineer and he was only a constable. Ainslie says it's because he's a Freemason. He says they do well for themselves at secret dinners. With their trousers rolled up? Probably, he said. Maybe that's why they wear pinnies. Pinnies? Aprons. Dirty eaters? Very likely, he said.

You don't see any European people in the club who aren't from the ships. The rest have gone.

When the Japanese came here in the war, the Europeans had to escape. Then about nine or ten years ago the Communists took over and that was really that for foreigners. The Mate says that nowhere in China is China. I think I know what he means. It's so big that Chinese in one part are so different that they speak almost a different language from Chinese in another part. Ah Ping [Chong Ah Ping, the ship's carpenter] says that most of the crew speak Cantonese. People in this part of China speak something different, sort of Mandarin. He says the one with the wart is trying to get all Chinese to speak the same language. How can he do that? It's like everyone where we come from having to speak French, or even English. He said, You belong India, you speakee English; you belong Africa, you speakee English. Maybe.

Chung, our chief steward, is Chinese. He doesn't go ashore here. He says he doesn't want trouble. I'm not sure what he means, but he certainly knows a lot about this place because his family come from here, not from Canton where most of the crew's families come from originally.

He says that his uncle was a very famous fortune-teller in Shanghai, and he told everyone what was going to happen. The steward says fortune-telling is still very important but dangerous because the new lot don't like it. According to him, Chinese fortune-telling is not one sort. It's like the people, always different. His uncle was the great expert (so he says) on something called Pa Kua, which he says is to do with the Book of Changes – which is what fortune-telling is, knowing what's going to change. I suppose that means our futures are not new. I said it was just like the stars in the newspapers. Maybe, he said. His uncle knew from lines on hands and faces and even by the way eyelids move. How did he know what was going to happen to China? He couldn't go round staring at hundreds of millions of eyelids. He said that was all in the stars. Was he right? The steward just looked over the side on to the dock. Very right. Very right. Perhaps that's why he won't go ashore. He knows what's going to happen next and doesn't want to be left behind.

All the Chinese crew are superstitious. Chong Ah Ping says the number four is unlucky because four people carry a coffin, and when you draw four in Chinese it looks like a coffin. I said, What happens if you have four children? He said, This fashion no good. Velly bad. I suppose you have to have another one quickly, but then I bet five's no good either.

He also says that cockroaches are good luck. It means that the house will have plenty of food. Maybe when the Mate tells us we have to paint the cabins with that stinking anti-cockroach stuff, I'll tell him it's bad luck to kill them. Then again, perhaps I won't.

## 12 MAY 1959, SHANGHAI

Saw the Second in the seamen's club. I think he's trying to have a drink at every stool at the bar. I wonder what happens to the snake when he's not there? No wonder the steward won't go in. I thought it was because he was a shirtlifter (the Second, that is, not the steward).

We're leaving first thing tomorrow. I'm sorry we're going. The Mate says it'll be good to get back to Hong Kong. Something about a good place to buy records. He's got a massive list of LPs he wants to buy. Odd. He hasn't got a record player. They don't work very well in a ta-fong.

## 13 MAY 1959, AT SEA BOUND FOR HONG KONG

The Fifth's come out in a rash. I heard the Chief having a go at the Third Mate. He said the Third Mate was trying to poison the Fifth. The Captain came down and said the best thing was to isolate the Fifth and give him plenty of sugar and water. That was this morning. The Old Man was on the bridge tonight and the Chief came up and said he'd better have a look at the Fifth. He's got a big bellyache and stripes over his back. The Mate says that's his sex habits with one of the donkeymen. I went round to see him when I came off watch tonight. He looked a bit grim, but I suppose that's because he's old. Old people never look good when they're ill. He said he was all right really and would be just fine if he could have a poop. I said that when I was small, Mum used to make me sit on the lav until I'd done it. One day I sat there for five hours and she only let me off because Dad refused to go in the garden again. Did you poop then, asked the Fifth. Oh yes, I said. I did ten minutes after I got on, but I wasn't going to tell her. I just sat there and read a whole Teddy Lester book. Twice. The Fifth said he'd try it. Sitting there, that is.

## 14 MAY 1959

Saw the Fifth this morning. Said he still hadn't had a poop. He was going to do what I suggested, but when he went along to the engineer's head the Third told him to push off because he'd got typhoid. Have you? Not as far as I know, he said. We'll be in Hong Kong tomorrow. They'll get a proper doctor to look at him. He asked me if I'd like to play crib. I said I had to study. The exam papers had to go off when we got in. I didn't really have to study. But suppose he really has got typhoid? I told Ainslie when I got back to the cabin. He said I had to have a shower and scrub everything. Did you touch him, he said. Course not. You sure? Course. Ainslie's a really nasty bit of work sometimes. I told him there was nothing much wrong with the Fifth except he couldn't poop. Ainslie said the Third Mate reckoned it was something he did when we were in Kobe. He said these woofters do strange things to each other. I got really angry then and said at least the Fifth hadn't got a hole in his mattress. He really got mad. What you mean by that? I didn't say anything, but he knew. I've heard him humping up and down in his bunk. I went back to see the Fifth just before I turned in. I said I'd give him a game of crib if he liked. He said not to bother. He wasn't feeling too hot. Maybe tomorrow.

# 12

## HOMEWARD BOUND

### 16 MAY 1959, HONG KONG

Back into Hong Kong and the Taikoo dock. They've got to cut out big chunks of the bow, including all the concrete, then re-plate. Then we'll have to have a survey. I reckoned we had the survey in that typhoon. The blokes who built this old tub in Scotland knew a thing or two.

They got the Fifth ashore and they say he's not coming back. I said, Does that mean he's dead? The Third Mate said, Oh no, not yet, anyway. He said this is a bit of an unlucky ship. Trip before last, the Captain went over the side. They were coming back from the States. Don't know why. But whatever it was, he just did. Just disappeared over the side.

## 17 May 1959, Hong Kong

I'm not feeling too bright. I keep getting a pain in my belly. Hope the Fifth didn't have something. I'm not sure if I should tell anyone.

## 18 May 1959, Hong Kong

I'm seeing the quack in the morning. Ainslie says I've always got to have something different. The Third Mate is a bit worried, because he's supposed to be the ship's doctor and he doesn't know. They've had enough trouble with the old Fifth, who I think everyone reckons is going to snuff it.

## 22 May 1959, Canossa Hospital

Two days ago I had my appendix out. I'm in the Canossa Hospital at Number 1 Peak Road. Dr Yeo said it was retroversal. Does that mean it was serious? Oh yes, he said. We got it just in time. I'm very glad it wasn't an ordinary appendix. I think Ainslie thought I was kidding and just wanted to get off the ship.

There's a wonderful old priest who's had some sort of operation. He wanders about in his white cassock, and about twice a day there's all sorts of laughing because he's got a bag and a tube into his belly because he can't pee properly. Suddenly the bag falls off and the nuns all fuss. He was telling me about Indo-China where he lives. He says there's so much corruption and so much killing. It's run by someone called Ngo Dinh Diem, who is a dictator. I said, Like the Castro bloke in Cuba. Oh no, he said. This Diem has no principles except his own. But, he said, that is the way of Asia. One day there will be a terrible war. Worse than the one they had before with his people – the priest is French.

## 1 June 1959, China Fleet Club

I'm now living in the China Fleet Club. I'm supposed to take it easy. All my gear's ashore. I saw Erricson's uncle and aunt today in Victoria. I said hello, but they just nodded and walked on. Didn't recognise me. I thought she might have done. When I came back here, I looked in the mirror. Perhaps I've changed. It's been a year. Interesting being ashore here instead of living on board. When you're on board, a run ashore is mostly shopping and a few beers. Now it's being part of the place. I quite like it. I was talking to someone who's like me, just out of hospital. He's from Texas, but he was born in Norwich. His dad was in the American air force during the war and his mother worked in Woolworth's. He said he's going to stay in Hong Kong. To do what? China coast? No fear, he said. Insurance. That's the thing. He's going for an interview tomorrow. I said I thought London was the place for insurance. He just laughed. So it is. But here you can really get rich. Hong Kong is going to be the richest place in the world ten years from now. Seems to know what he's talking about.

## 15 June 1959, China Fleet Club

They're flying me home next week. I've got to go back, take some medical leave and rejoin her when she gets to Europe. I don't know. I was thinking about Tex. He might be right. Perhaps it's time to do something else. Go to university or something. We'll see.

## 28 June 1959, home

Well, I'm here. Got a cab from the station. Bit different from when I went. All that humping about on the bus. As we came past the clock tower, I saw Bill Blackman, John Green and Phil Whaley and a couple of the others standing on the corner by Martin's Bank. I think they were standing there when I left.

I let myself in and the house was also just as it was. Except it feels empty. My bedroom's OK. Sort of, except I don't remember it being this tidy. Lot of things have gone. My scout's shirt and hat and my stave. Can't see my rugby things. I suppose that's OK. I shan't be staying. Thought I might at first. But not now. I think I've simply grown up in a different place.

The phone's off so I walked up to the Broadway and called the office. She's due into Dunkirk next month. Loading cars for Jacksonville, Fort Lauderdale and round to Pensacola, then up to Galveston to load scrap for Osaka. Then what? No one knew. That's fine.

Pop was waiting at the house for me when I got back. He said, Hello, then he said it, just as Ainslie said someone would: When you going back?

Bloody Ainslie.

# HISTORICAL NOTE

Conrad understood tramps. Not the gentlemen of the road but the old, often scruffy boat whose Master and agent bid for cargoes to carry anywhere in the world the vessels might go. Bales of jute. Bundles of pilgrims. Bit like the crews. A bundle of this and that. Highborn and lowlife. There was no telling until she sailed. It was all the same to bridge and office.

The tramp was the first cargo vessel. Even before the Phoenicians. It was, more often than not, a boat owned by its skipper. He offered himself and his boat for hire. There was probably no regular contract and so the skipper had to be willing to go anywhere. When he arrived, he hoped for a cargo to take home, or take on to another port. So he and his ship tramped from port to port. Later, some ships made regular runs to and from the same places. Overseas empires brought with them the need to resupply soldiers, families, officials and return with spoils. Much later, shipowners carried letters

– the parchments on which the great commercial empires were established and relied. Soon, the mail and regular-run ships had established timetables of supply lines between ports. So we had liners. But most ships were not so grand, weren't so favoured. Most ships and skippers still bartered and barged their skills for a bit of cargo here and another bit there. They still tramped from one port to another, from one merchant to another in search of a load. Sea-going carters is what they were. Willing to carry without many questions and usually not much profit.

Since the first sailing vessel there had always been an agent, an owner, a skipper tramping the watersides in search of business. In the earlier days, tramping was truly a taxi service inasmuch as the distances were rarely great. The vessel was small, and the skipper's knowledge of navigation and far-off places was scant. Sometimes, a roughly rigged vessel could pick up a trade wind and return on another or on a current. Many – no more than large yachts by today's standards – did not return at all. Skippers, sometimes bravely, sometimes foolishly, pressed further than they knew. The sea toyed with their peradventure, and many perished.

Sailors had left the Mediterranean for the Atlantic five hundred years before the birth of Christ. Celts and Phoenicians had reached as far as Greenland by AD 600. Overland traders had reached Cathay certainly by the twelfth century, and sailors could hug the coasts, pick up the monsoons and so on to the Far East. It was not until the sixteenth century that navigators made their deliberate ways to and from the Americas. The trade winds would take them from Europe; the Gulf Stream would bring them back.

By the eighteenth century, the seaways to Australasia and the Americas (on both coasts) were open. Yet even though the Industrial Revolution was recasting the silhouette of the commercial and social life of these islands, Britain's most important industry, the merchant vessel, sailed almost untouched until the 1840s.

On 21 October 1805, Nelson's fleet was victorious at the Battle of Trafalgar. The significance of that moment was that Britannia now felt confident that she ruled the waves. Throughout the whole Victorian era of empire and trade expansion, the British merchant fleet was pre-eminent in international trading. Great square-riggers, barques, barquentines, brigs and sleek schooners could sail unmolested wheresoever there was a cargo to be stowed and discharged. It would take more than another hundred years before the sea-lanes to and from the British Isles were threatened. During that time, the mercantile marine expanded like some great head of steam driving the nation's industrial and commercial wizardry across the world to wherever there was a port at which it might be unloaded for profit.

In no other nineteenth-century industry did the development of one simple principle of technology have so much effect. With the Industrial Revolution came the steam boiler that could drive the shaft that could turn the bronze propeller. Yet this was no revolution at sea. It was an evolution.

For it is a myth that the nation's prosperity was founded on the new maritime age of the steamship. Expanded, yes. Founded, no. Splendid paintings of steel-hulled Victorian steamers with thin funnels and black-bearded master mariners added to the romance of the age but did little for accurate accounts of the industrial history of the nation. It is certainly not true that once the steam engine had been built in the nineteenth century, then the sailing ship was finished. That was no more true than the jet engine meant the end of the aircraft propeller. Just as the propeller-driven Hercules cargo transport was still, at the start of the twenty-first century, the mainstay of the world's military transport fleets – more than half a century after the invention of the jet engine – so sail dominated maritime trade until well into the 1880s. For example, more than 250 British square-riggers were built during the 1880s and early 1890s. The *Mozart*, a four-masted barquentine, was built in 1904 and sailed between Chile and Germany on the lucrative nitrate run. In 1900 there were still two million tons of British shipping under sail, some of it not much changed in its principle of design for a century or more. Fine monuments to the famous British shipbuilder. Or were they? Ship-owners were never sentimentalists. Many British ships were built in Canada.

A lot of the timber used in British yards came from the Baltic. But this was heavily taxed. The Canadian builders (many of them had migrated from the British Isles) could often build more cheaply, and build lighter vessels, thanks to the use of plentiful seasoned softwoods. These ships were cheaper to buy and faster and therefore showed a better return on operating costs.

Yet it was not a shipowner's prudence that accounted for the slow development in the design of his vessels. In fact, during the first half of the nineteenth century, when so many industrial changes happened ashore, there was little change in the design of ships. The basic design of the vessel was difficult to fault and would remain on the drawing board until naval architects knew how to use steel and, most of all, had a new effective means of propulsion. From the single strength of a wherryman's paddle to the awesome consistency of a small nuclear reactor, a vessel's splendid lines are nothing without the means to power her. In the early nineteenth century that power was wind used by sails. Equally, the fine oils on canvas of ships slicing through force six seas are misleading. Mostly the sails in ships were of pretty poor fettle. The much-admired industrial changes ashore had not yet produced factory-woven sails. Most sails were loosely woven, soon baggy with wear and water and so soon inefficient. Shrouds and stays were still made of rope instead of spun wires. Altogether, ships may have been easy on the eye, but they were maritime hell to maintain.

Sailing ships leaked so much that aboard all but the very new ones the pumps were manned on every watch – six times a day. As a ship headed south into warmer latitudes, there was no let-up. Then the decks had to be kept wet otherwise the planks would shrink and the caulking come adrift. When the seas and rains came, water would get below and, truthfully, the rot would set in. The men who sailed in these vessels were not simply there to hand sails aloft. They spent most of their time keeping the vessel seaworthy. Chipping, scraping, splicing, mending and making. Even a modestly sized sailing ship would have hundreds of wooden blocks and miles of rope that had to be continuously checked. One worn fibre, one cracked block could dis-mast a vessel in high seas and storms, with all the imaginable consequences for crew, cargo and owner. Most of the ocean-going ships were small. Often vessels on the coastal trade were quite open. It was common for a sixty-foot sailing vessel to leave Britain bound for the Indian Ocean. The economics of such voyages are befuddling. But until the middle of the nineteenth century a 500- or 600-ton sailing ship (say, 120 to 130 feet long) was considered a large vessel.

So in the first half of the nineteenth century the shipping business was keeping pace with empire-building while, mostly, using ships that would have been easily recognisable in the eighteenth century. It was in the 1820s that the earliest steamships were to be seen trading in some limited form.

At first, steam power was used to drive paddles. The paddle steamer was sometimes used on mail runs (it was one of the few services willing to pay the enormous costs) as a ferryboat and as a very manoeuvrable tug – for sailing ships. It was not until the 1840s that a larger role for the steamer was developed, and even then it was in the coasting trade and it would be decades before the steamer would be ready to usurp the sailing ship.

This was the period of finding out for the engineers who were trying to produce the perfect maritime engine. The first aim was an efficient engine that could run for, say, ten to fifteen days on limited amounts of coal. It sounds simple. It was not. The object of the ship was to carry as much cargo as quickly as possible. The square-riggers did this very well. On the coastal trade, more conventionally rigged vessels – say, schooners or smacks – were easier to manoeuvre and could be handled by smaller crews.

The problem for the engineers was space and efficiency.

In the 1840s, producing a steam engine that could turn a propeller or, more likely, a pair of paddle wheels was not a difficult project. But how was that engine to be powered? Steam. How was the steam made? Firing water boilers by burning coal. Here was the first major difficulty. Where did they put the coal in a ship that was designed to make money from cargo, not coal? The space taken up by coal-bunkers was enormous. That space was needed for cargo, otherwise the voyage was unprofitable, unless, of course, the vessel was so fast that the turnaround times compensated for the high costs and small cargoes. This was rarely the case.

Furthermore, where were the steam vessels to get their coal? Bunker ports – coaling stations – had to be established along the route. This meant that early steamers could trade only where they could find coal or at either end of the voyage. This restricted them to the coastal trade and perhaps across the North Sea into the Baltic. An alternative for some owners was to find a regular trade for very expensive cargo (and not much of it) plus a few passengers. Then a ship could get further south, perhaps to the Mediterranean, where coal-bunkering could be set up relatively cheaply in, say, Gibraltar.

Curiously, it was the demand for coal – not on board, but ashore as factory and domestic fuel – that urged on the marine engineers. In the 1840s, much of that coal was still carried down the east coast of England aboard sailing colliers. It was a grand trade and centuries old. A hundred years earlier, in the 1740s, the eighteen-year-old James Cook had been bound apprentice to a sailing Master on the Yorkshire coast.

Even in those days, London was burning a million tons of coal a year. A thousand vessels were needed to carry that amount to the capital alone. The chances were that a round trip from, say, the Tyne would take a month. The collier might carry as much as 30 keels of coal – about 600 tons. By the 1840s, the demand was greater, the problem no less, the potential financial rewards remarkable. Remarkable men started on remarkable projects to gather those rewards.

When Charles Mark Palmer built the steam-collier *John Bowes* in his Jarrow yard in 1852, she cost £10,000. She was just short of 150 feet, with a beam of 26 feet, and she could carry 650 tons of coal. She could load that coal between breakfast and noon and be in London in two days. It would take another day to unload her (discharging cargo was always a more cumbersome and therefore slower process than loading and stowing) and then she'd be away and back on the Tyne in two days.

The *John Bowes* could do in less than a week what it would take the average sailing collier six or even seven weeks to do. Yet the engineering conundrum was far from resolved.

Many of the early steamships were less than stable. A steel hull can be loaded down with coal for its boilers and with bagged or bulk cargo. It will plough through quite heavy seas. But what happens when it's light ship, that is, without cargo? A sailing ship can load solid ballast, trim sails and even make better speed. A steel-hulled steamer has to be artificially balanced, which was a hit-and-miss affair and took time and therefore money – which was not at all what the steamship owners had in mind. The quick solution seemed to be the most obvious. Water. The *John Bowes*, for example, had water bags. They looked good on the drawing board, but not so good in practice. Too vulnerable. So the designers turned to steel ballast tanks.

The great advantage that steamships had over sailing ships at this stage (the 1840s and 1850s) was engine power that could drive not the ship but the pumps to load and discharge sea water into and from the ballast tanks. A man called John McIntyre worked in Palmer's Jarrow yard. In 1854 McIntyre designed a false bottom for a steamer called the *Samuel Laing*. Water could be pumped in and out of this double bottom in such a way that the ship was more than simply weighed down – it could be properly trimmed. From McIntyre's drawing board came the ideas that had to balance ships as they got bigger and carried more cargo and heavier loads – a hold full of wool obviously presents different trimming problems from even a half-full hold of iron ore. In principle, one problem is nearly solved. The major one – propulsion – was not.

The technology had not yet arrived that could drive ships by steam at a reasonable cost. There remained the uncertainties of failed engineering and scarce coaling stations. So it was hardly surprising that while many saw steam as the trade of the future, others concluded that it would be, for some time at least, best thought of as auxiliary power. So in the 1840s the idea took hold of having not one or the other, but a combination of sail and power. When the wind was good, use it; when it wasn't, then fire up the boilers. Any twenty-first century yacht is built on this principle, except that it's easy to switch on a modern yacht diesel, but it was not easy to fire a ship's boiler.

However, this dual role made a great deal of sense where it was difficult to get coal, for example on either side of Cape Horn – which was probably why big sailing Cape Horners bringing copper from South America remained viable until the early years of the twentieth century. In fact, for three-quarters of the nineteenth century there was no way in which the steamers could compete with the sailing ships on deep-sea voyages, particularly, for example, on the increasingly profitable and important long voyages to and from Australasia.

So what problems of marine engineering needed to be resolved if the tall ships were to be replaced?

In simple engineering, an engine had one cylinder with a piston inside and a boiler. The boiler had a fire stoked by coal. The heat from the fire heated water until steam was produced. The steam went into the cylinder, and its pressure drove the piston up and down. This up-and-down action turned a shaft. The shaft went along, horizontally, inside the ship until it emerged through a tube in the back (the stern) of the vessel. On the end of the shaft was the propeller. Or, in the early years, the tube went sideways, out through the hull and connected on either side of the vessel to paddle wheels. Very simple. Very inefficient.

As we have seen, ships simply did not have the space to carry the huge amounts of coal needed on long voyages where bunker facilities were hard to find and often expensive when they were available. Twenty per cent of the cost of a voyage could easily be taken up by coaling. It took until the 1850s for shipbuilders to realise that the answer, or at least the beginning of the answer, did exist but that it was not at sea. The answer was already working ashore.

Factories had sometimes used what were called compound engines. In the simplest terms a compound engine was one with not a single but with two cylinders and therefore two pistons. If a marine engineer could take a compound engine and use two cylinders to turn that propeller shaft, then – just like two men turning a handle – the job would be easier. Either two pistons would do less work to turn the shaft, or they could work equally hard and turn it more quickly.

The first option could easily be the better. The latter idea was based on more haste, but not that much more speed. A fast revolving shaft and, therefore, a faster-spinning paddle or propeller did not, in practice, always make the ship go that much quicker. Also, it could impose considerable strain on other bits and pieces of the structure and engineering. But simply using less effort to drive the propeller could mean less energy used and, therefore, less coal. It was not the price of coal that was important to the owner, but more frugal use allowed the ship to travel greater distances between bunkering ports. Longer voyages meant increased opportunities for trade – and thus more opportunities for profit.

Two men, John Elder and Charles Randolph, took the basic factory compound engine and designed a marine version. The first one appeared in a ship called the *Brandon* in 1854. She steamed using thirty per cent less coal than her predecessor, the *Carrick*. Other companies followed. By now the Peninsular and Oriental Steamship Company, P&O (whose name came from its mail services to the Iberian Peninsula and later to the Orient), needed to take every advantage of modern marine engineering to maintain its ambitions on long-haul voyages to the Far East. In 1861 P&O installed the first of its compound engines into the *Mooltan*.

However, this was not enough. The boilers could not produce enough pressure, and the pistons were too slow. Steam is 'made' in a condenser. Anyone who has tried to pump up a bicycle tyre knows the difference between a good pump and an old-fashioned one that takes ages to get the tyre hard. It's more or less the same principle with a marine engine. Low steam coming in at low pressure means the pistons won't work very hard.

In the early days (the 1840s and 1850s), a ship's engineer was lucky to get more than thirty pounds per square inch of steam into the cylinders. To really get those pistons going, the boilers needed twice that amount. Gradually, the designers learned how to modify the condenser and so increase the pressure. From just thirty pounds it was squirting into the cylinders at twice that amount by the 1860s and even more (seventy pounds per square inch) by the 1870s. The other breakthrough was the type of steel used to build the boilers. Very high pressures needed stronger steel. The development of high-quality mild steel made all the difference in the world. Indeed, it had a worldwide result.

A man in Liverpool called Alfred Holt was an engineer, and a very clever one, who had started his own shipping line, the Ocean Steam Ship Company. In the twenty-first century, perhaps such a title doesn't mean very much. But think in terms of the early nineteenth century. Here we are, easily in living memory of Nelson and the Battle of Trafalgar, with tall masts, spars, top gallants and lower courses seen in every estuary, strait and seaway, and now we have a company trading out of the Mersey called Ocean Steam Ship. In those three words, Alfred Holt saw the maritime future. Of course, Holt was not the first. Even a few of those early names suggests the excitement in the mercantile marine, particularly the transatlantic trade.

In 1819 we already had the Savannah Steam Ship Company in America. There was the Valentia Transatlantic Steam Navigation Company, and in 1838 the City of Dublin Steam Packet Company. In 1850 the New York & Liverpool United States Mail Steam Ship Company and the Inman & International Steamship Company Limited. In 1854 the Clyde Screw Steam Packet Company, the

General Screw Steam Shipping Company and the London & Limerick Steamship Company. These are a very few of the shipping companies, often with just one vessel, that were launched with the beginning of steamers. Their owners were energetic pioneers determined to break from the warps and springs of sail. The Atlantic Ocean was the obvious test of these pioneers. It was, after all, the frontier, the shipowners' Oregon Trail.

The first steamship to cross the Atlantic was the *Savannah*. The date: 1819.

On 7 May 1818 a notice appeared in the *Savannah Gazette* in Georgia announcing that a company had been formed with capital of $50,000. It was called the Savannah Steam Ship Company. At the same time, up in New York a boat yard was run by two men, William Crockett and Samuel Fickett. Crockett and Fickett were then building a wooden sailing ship. She was 300 or so tons and went into the water during the third week of August that year, 1818. That ship – designed for the coastal trade – was bought by a mariner called, Moses Rogers. Rogers was the brains (although not the money) behind the Savannah Steam Ship Company, and the new vessel was named the *Savannah*. So we have a ship but no engines.

In New Jersey three more pioneers – James Allaire, Stephen Vail and Daniel Dod – were building an engine and boilers. The engine was simple, with a single cylinder about the same size as a short and chubby man (around forty inches in diameter and five feet tall). To run that engine, they built a pair of boilers made of copper. Each one was twenty-six feet tall and six feet wide. This was mammoth marine engineering in those days. It was the simplest illustration of the enormous energy needed to run a small engine during the first part of the nineteenth century. Now they had to decide what should be done with the engine. Their answer: paddles, each sixteen feet in diameter.

The original plan for the Savannah Steam Ship Company was to open the transatlantic trade to steam. It should have been a very exciting moment for the general public – almost the maritime equivalent to the first jet flight. It was not. In May 1819 the company ran an advertisement in the *Daily Georgian* offering berths to passengers aboard the *Savannah* on 20 May – just a couple of days after the advertisement appeared. Perhaps it really was too short notice. Perhaps no one trusted the vessel. Perhaps no one wanted to go to Liverpool. For that's where the *Savannah* was bound – Savannah, Georgia, to the Mersey. She sailed empty – not even any cargo. On the early-morning tide of 24 May 1819, the *Savannah* weighed anchor off the Tybee Light. Nearly a month later, she arrived in the Mersey at six o'clock in the evening of 20 June. Of the twenty-nine days, some hundred hours had been under steam. The rest of the time she'd sailed. As a reminder of the difficulty facing steamship owners, the *Savannah*'s log shows that she had to wait five days in St George's Channel for coal supplies.

The *Savannah* was not a success. The king of Sweden, Charles XIV, offered to buy her. The tsar of Russia, Alexander I, wanted the ship and her master and crew to stay in the Baltic. But they wouldn't. She was sailed home, again empty and stripped of boilers and engine. She reverted to what Fickett and Crockett had said she was, a sailing packet, and for a couple of years she sailed between Savannah and New York before being wrecked, appropriately, off Fire Place, Long Island. It was a sad end to the first steamship to sail the Atlantic.

In London a company called American and Colonial Navigation was formed in 1825. This was the first proper scheme to establish a transatlantic steamship line, rather than simply run across the Atlantic to prove that it could be done under, or with the help of, steam. American and Colonial reckoned they needed to build ships that could do the trip in under a fortnight. The idea seems to have been to use not Liverpool but Valentia in south-west Ireland as the base for the regular run between Great Britain and the American eastern seaboard. Valentia is still famous. It is heard every few hours towards the end of the shipping forecast when they get to the reports from coastal stations. '. . . Channel Light Vessel Automatic, Land's End, Valentia, Ronaldsway including the waters around Carlingford Lough . . .' Romantic enough now, but at that time Valentia, or sometimes Valencia, was to be the gateway to the Atlantic.

From Ireland to New York, from Ireland to St John's, Newfoundland, and then to Halifax, Nova Scotia. From Ireland to the Leeward Islands, then Jamaica, then back via the Azores. Why Valentia? The answer is really a lump of coal – or many thousands of lumps. From south-west Ireland to St John's, Newfoundland, is less than 2,000 miles. The steamship owners believed they could just do this with an 800-ton ship carrying 200 tons of profitable cargo, a few passengers and simply loads and loads of coal. It didn't happen.

It was not until the late 1830s that the first workable plans to set up a transatlantic service came to anything.

The story now turns to the British & American Steam Navigation Company and two men, Junius Smith, an American, and Isaac Solly, sometime chairman of the LBR, the London and Birmingham Railway. Smith had travelled to Europe aboard a sailing ship. The voyage took fifty-seven days. This was in the 1830s. Steam was a reality, not a sailor's dream. Smith had fifty-seven days in which to ponder how crazy it was that anyone (including him) would (or had to) spend close on two months to get to Europe. So he tried to start a steam shipping company of his own.

In the summer of 1835, Junius Smith published a prospectus trying to raise £100,000. There was no interest. It was not that people were blind to the idea of transatlantic steaming; it simply wasn't ambitious enough. So that October, he tried again. He upped the capital investment to £500,000 and published the name of the proposed company: British & American Steam Navigation Company. This attracted Isaac Solly.

Solly's influence as a railwayman was exactly what the project needed, and soon people were putting their money into the B&A. It's worth remembering that this was only thirty years since the Battle of Trafalgar. The maritime image can hardly have been different even though the memory in Britain, and therefore among investors, had not once dimmed. A year later, in 1836, they ordered their first ship, a 2,000-ton wooden paddle steamer. She was to be called the *Royal Victoria*, but between ordering and building, William IV died and the eighteen-year-old Victoria came to the throne. Smith and Solly changed the ship's name and, they hoped, her profile. She would be called the *British Queen*. The ship was building in Curling & Young's yard on the Thames, but the engines were coming from Glasgow – or were supposed to. The engineers, Claude Girdwood, ran out of money. Another Glasgow engineer, Robert Napier, realised that British & American were determined to be the first transatlantic company with a regular steamer run. It didn't take much gossip among the clubs and exchanges to know that others were trying to do the same. So Napier said that he could and would deliver the engines, but they would cost a lot more and wouldn't be ready for another year. Smith and Solly had little choice. They ordered the new engines.

Then came news that another group just formed in Bristol, called the Great Western Steam Ship Company, was building a rival ship called the *Great Western*. Moreover, she was nearly ready for sea trials. This was no ordinary rival.

A couple of years earlier there had been a board meeting of Great

Western Railway. The Paddington to Bristol line was not then open (it did, in 1841). But the GWR Chief Engineer was Isambard Kingdom Brunel. At that meeting, he apparently suggested that instead of stopping at Bristol, the GWR should run from London to New York. That was in October 1835. By March the following year, the Great Western Steam Ship Company was formed and Brunel set about with Christopher Claxton (a Royal Naval lieutenant who was appointed managing director) to design their first ship, not surprisingly to be called the *Great Western*.

Imagine the gloom in the British & American boardroom and trading rooms. All this work, investment and planning. It was true that there was more than enough room for everyone in the Atlantic. But here we find two elements of our story which keep repeating themselves right into the twentieth century: determination and innovation, the qualities of the pioneering spirit that was found in the covered waggon stories and soon in the great American railway tale. In the nineteenth century and the opening decades of the twentieth this spirit would be found at sea. That sense of being a physical, not just an intellectual pioneer was the element of business and technology that had gone by the late twentieth and early twenty-first centuries. In 1837, the year in which Victoria came to the British throne, Smith and Solly were determined not to be second. The answer was neither on the dockside nor in the engineer's yard, but in the boardroom. When the company had been formed, some of the directors were also directors of something called the Saint George Steam Packet Company, which was running small ships between the Thames and southern Ireland. Their new ship, the 703-ton *Sirius*, was just being fitted out. She was the answer, or at least seemed to be. Smith and Solly chartered the *Sirius*, and on 28 March she sailed from London with twenty-two passengers. On the way down the Thames, there was the *Great Western* working up for the same trip. The race was on.

The two-masted *Sirius* put in at Cork, embarked seventy or so more passengers, no cargo but enough coal to get her across the Atlantic. It was to be an eventful voyage, with the Captain reportedly threatening to shoot crew members who demanded he turn back when they hit bad weather. On 22 April she finally made New York, just a few hours ahead of the *Great Western* – which in fact was a faster ship. The gamble and the charter had paid off – almost. The British & American Steam Navigation Company had become the first to start a transatlantic steamer service. But the *Sirius* was never designed for this trade. She was too small and too expensive to operate as a charter vessel.

Eventually, the *British Queen* was ready and caused quite a stir. After all, here, with her three masts, sails, thin funnel amidships and huge paddle wheels, was the biggest steamship the world had ever seen. She was a little over 1,800 tons, which by later standards was tiddly (the twentieth century super-tankers were often 250,000 tons and sometimes twice that size), although well under 10,000 tons was the norm right through the nineteenth century. The *British Queen*, with 200 and more passengers (her dining saloon measured sixty feet by thirty feet), could make the transatlantic voyage in about two weeks. Sailing packets were often taking five weeks for the outward voyage and three or four weeks for the homeward trip,* and some ships were in theory making a small profit. However, it didn't take much to shred the balance sheet. The *British Queen*'s sister ship, the *President*, was lost at sea (commanded by Lieutenant Roberts of the Royal Navy, who had commanded the *Sirius* during the original voyage), and no amount of small profit-taking could cope with the

*The difference is due to prevailing winds going out and picking up the Gulf Stream coming back to Europe.

consequences. By the 1840s the pioneer of transatlantic steamer trade had folded. The *Great Western* carried on and was joined in 1845 by her sister ship, a vessel that was to become, in the United Kingdom at least, as famous as HMS *Victory*. She was called the *Great Britain*, although that wasn't the original idea.

Brunel wanted to build an iron ship. Until now, big ships were wooden. Most ships were. Brunel could see all the advantages of iron but failed to convince any shipbuilder that he might be right. So Great Western had to dig their own dry dock. The ship was going to be called the *Mammoth*, which seemed the most suitable name for the first ocean-going iron steamer, especially as she was 3,270 tons. Originally, she would have been a paddle steamer like her predecessors, but Brunel had seen another ship with a propeller. He thought about it. Drew it. Thought about it again and then abandoned the paddles. So the *Great Britain*, as the *Mammoth* was now called, was the first iron and propeller-driven ocean steamer. Everyone thought her tremendous. Big. Prestigious. Five years from keel to maiden voyage. Yet she was never much of a sailing success on the transatlantic trade. Great Western sold her. At various times she was laid up, rebuilt and spent many years running between Liverpool and Australia. Towards the end of her deep-sea life, her engines were taken out and she was rigged as a sailing ship and eventually used in the Falkland Islands as a coal and wool hulk until she was 'rescued' in the 1960s and returned to Bristol, where her story had begun.

Our story is now in the middle of the nineteenth century and we come back to Alfred Holt, whose name would survive into twenty-first century shipping.

At this point, remember that Holt was an engineer by trade. Now, in the 1860s, he designed his own compound engines. This single development made his company, Ocean Steam Ship, and his

Blue Funnel Line that followed, one of the most important and innovative shipping companies on the maritime exchanges.

There were two great advances: his own design of what was called a tandem compound engine, and better boilers. A tandem compound engine simply meant lining up the engines to work together – a bit like a tandem bicycle. One person in front, one behind, and life's that much easier. Same with engines – especially if you're trying to drive a propeller. The second development was in the plumbing department – the boiler and the condenser.

Once boilers were made from improved mild steel, they could stand more pressure. More pressure means that the pistons can really get going. So can the ship. To get the steam, super-heated water had to go through the condensers – to be condensed to steam. In the early days, salt water was pumped through. Of course, the whole thing too easily clogged up. Just think what it must have been like trying to cross the Atlantic and having to stop after four days to unclog the tubes – which is what happened. What was the answer? Obvious. Fresh water. The ship's engineers could do two things: make fresh water by recycling the steam, which at the time was not efficient, or carry fresh water. If a ship had efficient engines, then it didn't need so much bunker space for coal so could carry more cargo. With bottom tanks (which needed space), a ship could carry water. The vessel didn't have to be stopped mid-Atlantic; it was therefore safer, faster and so more profitable.

Alfred Holt had an old steamer called the *Cleator*. She was hardly an ocean greyhound. Most of the time she'd been used on the coal and iron ore run between the north-west coast of England and South Wales. Holt stripped out her engine and put in his new one, the tandem, and the increased boiler pressure. It worked. There was an immediate forty per cent saving on fuel, which meant the *Cleator* could sail further than ever imagined for her. Very soon, she was making the trip to South America.

Holt then put his new propulsion system in three new ships, the three As – *Ajax*, *Achilles* and *Agamemnon* – and so started the Ocean Steam Ship Company. Liverpool to the Orient: a long way in 1860. Nine years later it was 3,600 miles nearer because that was the year, 1869, in which the Suez Canal opened, knocking at least ten days off the journey – that's almost three weeks on the round trip. In theory, it could have been faster, but probably a day and a half was always lost waiting to join the convoy, getting the Canal lights fitted to the bow for a night passage, and waiting in the Bitter Lakes to let the convoy coming the other way get through. But it was still profitable even with the high toll charges for transit through the waterway.

While Holt's ships did well out of the engineering phenomenon, others did not. If there was a single moment when the giant tea clippers knew they were on the way out, it was the opening of the 103-mile-long Suez Canal. Equally, this was also the year in which the *Cutty Sark* was launched. She was more than two hundred feet long, with a beam of thirty-six feet, and had three great masts, the main (the middle one) more than a hundred and forty-five feet tall, and on a fair day two dozen sails set.

On her maiden voyage, she loaded tea in Shanghai on 25 June 1870. On 12 October she was sighted off Beachy Head. The *Cutty Sark* had made the voyage in just 109 days. The next year, on her second voyage, she sailed from Shanghai on 4 September and picked up the North Foreland light 107 days later on 20 December. She'd never make a faster passage. On her final tea voyage, in 1877, she loaded tea at Hankow and sailed from Woosung on 6 June. It took her 122 days before she picked up the Scillies. Now here is some idea of the timescale and the importance of steam development.

Even the great clippers like the *Cutty Sark* and her rival, the *Thermopylae*, couldn't do more than one round trip a year. The *Cutty Sark* was taken off the tea trade in 1877. She went tramping. Jute from Manila to New York, coal from Wales to Japan for the American navy. Now they were voyages of Conradian proportions. The pride of the China tea fleet riddled with the grisly drama of the rough tramp.

It began in the Indian Ocean, when the Mate murdered one of the deckhands with a marlin spike. The Mate escaped the authorities when the *Cutty Sark* anchored. The crew didn't actually mutiny but came close to it. The Captain, who had only just taken command because his predecessor had died at sea, went to pieces and stepped over the side into a school of sharks in the Java Sea. The owner, John Willis, sent the Mate of the *Hallowe'en*, a man called Bruce, to take command. The *Cutty Sark* carried on tramping. New York, Sydney, the Philippines, Shanghai, Calcutta, Melbourne. So very different from the great days of loading in Hankow and then racing for the Lizard against the *Thermopylae*. Nevertheless, all should have been well. All was not well.

Cholera laid low the hands in Shanghai. Two died and one, a young boy, had to be returned to London. In Melbourne a sailor fell from the foremast and drowned. Another fell overboard at sea and was never seen again. So perhaps it was little wonder that with all this loss of life and not forgetting two dead captains and a stabbed deckhand, Captain Bruce was by now convinced that the ship was haunted. He took to drink and prayer meetings.

By 1883 Bruce was gone and so was the *Cutty Sark* from the tramping trade, for a decade anyway. She, and other ships in Willis's fleet, went on the wool run between England and Australia. With fine weather, she could make the 11,000-or-so-mile trip in less than seventy days. She made twelve wool runs between 1883 and 1895, and then she was sold – to a Portuguese company – renamed the *Ferreira* and again became a tramp. Down to Rio and up to the Gulf of Mexico and New Orleans. She kept going, although re-rigged as a schooner during the Great War and was eventually sold off in 1922 as a moored training hulk in Devon – more than half a century after her launching into a 'dying' trade.

So now we come to the twentieth century. We have come to the times of Conrad and Kipling, for the story of the tramp is also the story of Britain's colonial history. The times when shipping was strong, when the red ensign flew at the stern of most ships in almost any port anywhere in the world. The times when British shipping had faded and the ensign was usurped by the blues, reds, greens, yellows and whites of Panama, Liberia and Monrovia were the times when the colonial façade crumbled before the wind of change.

At the start of the twentieth century, more than half the world's shipping flew the red ensign. Sixty per cent of those ships were tramps. They steamed at an unhurried eight, nine or ten knots as stokers shovelled ton after ton of good Natal coal into the boilers. Three great piston engines, each the height of a tall house, turned the wide-bladed propeller that left a hundred-year wake from Rio to Shanghai to Panama, from the Baltic to the Bass Strait. Yet most of the tramps were never part of grand fleets. Yeomen, not aristocrats. Take, for example, the old *Saint* boats.

Back in the 1850s there was a man called Robert Rankin. He had a few wooden sailing ships running out of Liverpool to North America. In the early 1860s he took on a partner by the name of Gilmour. So the company became known as Rankin and Gilmour, and within twenty years they had six iron sailing ships and an office in South John Street in Liverpool. They named all their ships *Saint* something or other. They were still in sail when others were in steam. Rankin and Gilmour went to see another man in Liverpool by the name of Royden who had a shipyard. In 1880 Royden built them three steam tramps, the *Saint Albans*, the *Saint Bernard* and the *Saint Columba*. Over on the Tyne, another company, called Andrew Leslie, built the *Saint Dunstan*. Rankin liked the building on the Tyne, and in 1886 the Tyneside yard Armstrong Mitchell built the *Saint Oswald*. By the end of the century Rankin and Gilmour had ordered thirty steam tramps. They changed their name to the British and Foreign Steam Ship Company Limited. Then, in 1919, the company became the Saint Line.

Some of the ships were sold on; others, like the *Saint Pancras*, perished at sea. One of them, the *Saint Kilda*, was sunk by Russian warships in the China Sea in 1905. The *Kilda* was loaded with jute and cotton on passage to Yokohama. Why would the Russians do that? They were at war with the Japanese, and anybody trading with Japan was fair game for the remnants of a Russian fleet humiliated and eventually destroyed by the Japanese. She wasn't the only one to go down in war. The *Saint Egbert* sailed in 1914 from Colombo loaded with sugar for New York. She had only got as far as Cape Comorin in the Indian Ocean when she was intercepted by a German cruiser, the *Emden*. In 1916 a German U-boat sank the *Saint Ursula* forty-five miles south of Malta. In 1917 the *Saint Theodore* and the *Saint Ronald* were both sent to the bottom.

After the Great War trading times were hard and by the start of the Depression at the end of the 1920s the Saint Line was running out of money. In the 1930s the once-modest fleet was reduced to the *Saint Dunstan* and the *Saint Andrew*. The great change came in 1937, when the company was sold to the overseas trading company Mitchell Cotts. By the start of the Second World War the Saint Line and its sister company, the Sun Shipping Company, had just six vessels. German torpedoes did for five of them. Only the *Saint Bernard* survived. After the war there was trade to be done. Always would be, they judged, and so the company started to rebuild. There were ships enough. There was life in them and the small companies, but not much. The Saint Line would try its best. Famous names would once more be registered at Lloyd's: the *Saint Bernard*, the *Saint Dunstan* and the smartest of them all, the *Saint Gregory*. But it couldn't last. The Saint Line's story was hardly unique. She was a colony in Britain's mercantile empire. Like many imperial fortunes, she was vulnerable, not to political and social change, but to the costs of progress.

Bulk carriers appeared. Then containers. There came, too, the new technologies. Now a ship could sail, pick up and discharge a cargo with a dozen crew instead of sixty. Finally came the accountants and lawyers. Owners flagged their ships in Panama and Liberia. The crews were cheaper, the regulations less demanding. And so by the 1950s the old 7,000-ton tramps were finding fewer cargoes. With their passing, so went the British shipping industry as generations had known it. The strong, dark polished offices in Leadenhall Street began to close. So, too, did the British Empire.

No more Conrad.